ACROSS the KITCHEN TABLE

ACROSS the KITCHEN TABLE

talking about

TRANS

with your teen

—— SAM A. ANDREADES ——

Across the Kitchen Table
Talking about Trans with Your Teen
Sam A. Andreades

Unless otherwise noted, Scripture quotations are from the ESV® (The English Standard Version®), copyright © 2001 by Crossway, a publishing ministry of Good News Publishers. Used by permission. All rights reserved.

Copyright © 2023, Sam A. Andreades

All rights reserved. No part of this book may be reproduced, scanned, or distributed in any printed or electronic form without permission.

ISBN: 979-8-9889992-5-6

Cover photo: Mary K. A. Andreades
Back cover photo: Ryan Estes
Cover design: www.greatwriting.org

IN OUR IMAGE

There is no conversation more important than this one, and no book more helpful in forging it. Before one more child is lost to the alienation and deception of the transgender phenomenon, please buy and read this book. Pastor Andreades demystifies this politically charged debate, bringing pastoral care and Scripture to bear on its heartfelt questions. This is a must-read. I recommend this book to every Christian home.

—ROSARIA BUTTERFIELD: Author, *The Secret Thoughts of an Unlikely Convert* and *The Gospel Comes with a House Key*

Most of the church is woefully ill-prepared to respond to the many pressing challenges posed by the "trans" phenomenon. Sam Andreades' latest book, *Across the Kitchen Table*, will help equip you to do so with great charity and great clarity. With keen insight and sound counsel, Andreades places today's confusion about the body and gender exactly where it belongs: in the context of our creation, fall, and redemption. In the process, he shows us that true hope lies not in the technological promise of salvation from our bodies, but in the biblical promise of the salvation of our bodies.

—CHRISTOPHER WEST, ThD.: Author, *Our Bodies Tell God's Story: Discovering the Divine Plan for Love, Sex, and Gender*

Across the Kitchen Table was an absolute privilege to read. There were so many "This section is great" places I highlighted in yellow, topics addressed by someone who has really thought through these matters deeply in conjunction with many experiences in ministering to people.

This book is meeting a huge demand. I'm just glad that I now have a go-to resource to send desperate parents to. I'll definitely be having our staff read it as well because I'm sure we'll be referring back to this book time and time again. I know this labor of love will be used for the benefit of so many families who are in such desperate need.

—MARK SANDERS: President of Harvest U.S.A.

What Sam has written is a much needed resource. It's not a word-for-word guide for what to say to your children struggling with gender or declaring a trans or non-binary gender identity. Rather, it's a tool to know how to respond to whatever your children might say, laying a foundation of truth from Scripture and general revelation. His flowchart for navigating the different types of gender confusion is invaluable. And he has unearthed some real gems from the Bible that are desperately needed in this discussion, giving insights to buttress against potential "got ya" rebuttals and doubts that our children may voice.

—ANDREW RODRIGUEZ, MS, LPC: Integrity Christian Counseling

Thanks

I would like to thank Mary K. A. Andreades, Andrew Gess, Karen B. Lacy, Andrew Rodriguez, and Mark Sanders for pre-reading the manuscript and offering helpful comments, to Goodwill Media for its strong help in bringing this project to fruition, and to the many people whose personal stories are described herein, from whom I have learned so much.

Sam A. Andreades, August, 2023

Contents

Introduction 11
1 A Trans Diagnostic Flowchart 13

BODY

2 An Old Experience, A New Term 27
3 Our Bodies Are Who We Are 33
4 Where Our Dysphoria Comes From 41
5 "How Long Has He Been Like This?" 47
6 Sometimes We Are Wrong About Ourselves 55
7 The Way Home 63

BREATH

8 Desires Are Moral 71
9 Rediscovering Gender 79
10 Valuing Woman 87
11 Beckoning Man 93
12 The Stutterer Orator 103

BATTLE

13 Psycho-Medical Science, History, and the History of the Science 113
14 Battling Against the Body 123
15 A Message to the Church: The Last Shall Be First ... 129
Conclusion 135

Endnotes 143
Bible Book Name Abbreviations 152
Index of Scriptures Referenced 153

Across the Kitchen Table

Introduction

Notes from a Pastor's Desk

Many different voices now confront us about how to understand distress about one's body and gender. As this pastor has taught and counseled people about gender issues for many years, he found the Bible to be an invaluable guide to navigate these rough waters of transgenderism. You are reading the biblical principles he arrived at in helping those he loves, written down so you can gain confidence in helping those you love. These are notes from his desk.

While he also consulted with licensed counselors in their valuable work, researched the social science literature for its important insights, and engaged with Western culture's puzzling trends, the dearth this minister saw was in this kind of pastoral counsel. This biblical-pastoral book is for parents and their teens who want to know how to address the trans-phenomena as they impact their home. You don't have to be a professional. You don't need a special degree. God does not leave you adrift in navigating these waters.

Rather, you have a puzzle to solve. What follows are most of the big pieces. As we lay these large principles out on the kitchen table and talk about how to talk about them with our loved ones, I hope you will be able to see the big picture. While discussing one piece (chapter), I will at times refer to others at the places where they fit together, with the notation {Piece #}. I hope thereby to give you a framework of the scene before you. You can then fill in the smaller pieces of your own family situation. But, be prepared. The Bible's truths about gender confront us deeply about our own lives as well as those we may be trying to help. Gender is a journey for all of us. Expect this to be a growing experience for you as well as your teen.

The first Bible book, *Genesis,* presents to us the beginnings of the world we know. Before even that beginning, the book's first two chapters recall moments before the world we know, back when God called it all good. It is a glimpse into that misty time when things were done right, before the account of humanity's cosmic fall. I often wish those first two chapters were longer, that they said more. Like whether, in that bright time, they squeezed the toothpaste tube in the middle or at the back, or what was the best form of government. But they don't. The author relays the most salient points for us to understand about our world and ourselves.

A big portion of the precious account of beginnings is the description of the creation of gender. And the report reaches a climax in a simple statement about the new humanity, before our great tumbling into sin. What is the text's conclusion of that time of "all good"? It is this:

> And the man and his wife were both naked and were not ashamed.[a]

Understanding trans begins with understanding that statement.

a Gen 2:25.

1

A Trans Diagnostic Flowchart

Across the Kitchen Table

You sit there bewildered. Across the kitchen table, your young'un has just declared, "I am queer non-binary," or "This body is not who I am." You did not think your family was that messed up, but this is throwing you for a loop. Once again, you feel out of your league in this whole parenting thing.

Or, that scene has not happened. But, perhaps a friend has confessed to your teen that he or she is trans. Your child is asking you how to respond. You are at a loss. Or, an uncle has begun estrogen treatments and is asking your family to use a new name for him. How do you advise your child on engaging with him? Or, is it her? How do you even interpret the request? How do you raise your young person in the midst of the now-prevalent trend in the culture?

Or, maybe you have seen some clothing in a drawer that stopped you in your tracks. You are putting two and two together and realizing that the child you thought you knew has begun leading a double life. At school, your child has taken on a different persona and the school authorities have not informed you, out of a fear that you wouldn't understand what your child needs. You know you belong in the equation, but feel intimidated by the professionals. How do you win back your kid?

Or, savvy parent that you are, you perceive the enormous cultural changes taking place and you want to know how to teach your younger children on what they are about to encounter just outside your door.

Transgenderism is a big umbrella of a term, covering many conditions and experiences. Thus, a parent or teacher of a teen who stands under it needs a flowchart to get to the heart of what is really going on. Let's build such a chart for our first piece of the puzzle.

First Responders

Your first response when confronted with trans leanings is critical. Before understanding, the beginning note to sound as a parent is acceptance in love. This is not a comprehensive book about how to parent. (It would be much longer!) But, of course, we are talking here and throughout the book about good parenting. These first moments are the time to say things like, "Honey, I love you and will always love you." And, "I want to walk with you through this next phase of your life." And, "I'm very happy that you've told me what is going on with you." And, "You mean so much to me."

Affirming your love is not an agreement with your teen's interpretation of things. You are only properly prioritizing the relationship. The apostle tells us that we grow to maturity as we speak the truth in love to one another.[a] The truth will come. Start with the love.

Affirm Your Love

> Affirm Your Love

But then you still need to figure out what is going on beneath the word. I recommend holding five boxes in your mind as you listen and explore. Use these categories to decide what kind of trans confronts you and how to help.

Boxes Your Teen May Be In

A) A Craving to Fit In

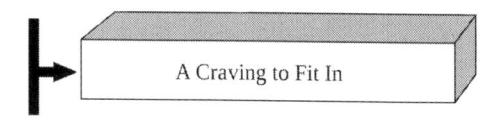

> A Craving to Fit In

We all desire to be accepted by our peers but, for teenagers, the desire is visceral. In this vulnerable time of life, what one's friends think often looms large. Life may feel desperately lonely. The need to be cool with

a Eph 4:15.

one's companions powers what is being called *rapid onset gender dysphoria*,[1] which is not really a gender dysphoria at all. Instead, the term showcases what any parent of teen girls already knows: connection with friends can create conditions of illness. Their empathy easily swirls into social contagion. If it has become fashionable in your neighborhood to go trans, your teen may not want to miss out.

If your teen is in this box, the solution is the same as it has always been from time immemorial. The book of *Proverbs* reminds us, in the father's repeated and impassioned pleas to choose his own counsel over that of his son's companions,[a] that the teen years are a battle for your child's heart. Whether the competing companion voices come from clueless friends, professional groomers, or the furious Zeitgeist we call the Internet, the task of every parent is to win the affectionate respect of their developing child. Detoxing from social media helps a lot. But, even more importantly, you should take this as a call to renew your relationship. The quality of your bond with your child in the teen years will make the biggest difference in what happens next.

B) A Lurking Comorbidity

⊢→ A Lurking Comorbidity

a Pro 1:8–10, 1:15, 4:10–19, 5:1–23, 6:20–24, 7:1–5, 23:15–17, 23:19–22, 23:26–27, 24:13–22, 28:7.

If it is not just a thirst for peer favor, then we need to be open to more serious problems. Possibly, a mental health or personality disorder hides under the cross-gender desire. Autism, depression, and anxiety disorders are common such co-occurring concerns, called comorbidities.

Tim was a skinny guy and always way out there according to his friends. ("Tim" is not his actual name. All names used in this book are changed, but their stories are quite real.) When trans got popular, he thought that this was the answer for sure. He adopted the persona of "Ann" and took female hormones for a year. But Tim was also honest, which led to thoughtful self-reflection. As his instability continued, he realized that his real problem was being masked by the trans stuff.

Many studies show such co-occurring conditions. The first systematic study done on the connection between gender dysphoria and autism was published in 2010. It found the incidence of autism among gender dysphoric children to be ten times higher than the rate in the general population.[2] People who work in gender clinics are well aware of this connection. Measured over an eighteen-month period at Great Britain's Gender Identity Development Service, more than half of the young people with gender dysphoria showed features of autism.[3]

A 2003 Dutch survey reported in the *American Journal of Psychiatry* found 61 percent of gender dysphoric patients had other psychiatric illnesses, notably personality, mood, dissociative, and psychotic disorders, to which the cross-gender desires were secondary.[4] (This percentage is low, based on how they measured it.) A 2014 study published by the *British Journal of Psychiatry* gathered results from a multi-center survey in four European countries.

They found that, even in those trans-accepting nations, gender dysphoric persons show many more psychiatric difficulties than the general population. Seventy percent, in fact, had a current and lifetime diagnosis.[5] A 2009 review from Case Western Reserve University found nine out of their clinic cohort of ten had at least one other significant form of psychopathology.[6] This is why psychologists who used to treat gender dysphoria as symptom rather than cause often succeeded in resolving the feelings.[7]

If this is our box, we likely already know it as we have been living with our child. It is wise to address the problem on multiple fronts: probably therapy or some type of additional care counseling, possibly medication, definitely spirituality—engaging with the powerful truths of the gospel. The New Testament advises that we should also not dismiss demonic activity as a consideration.[a]

C) *True Body Alienation*

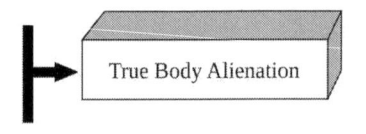

If your teen really does experience a singular and intense body distress, it is most likely due to earlier trauma in life. After decades of experience, two of the psychologists instrumental in Great Britain's recent course reversal in the treatment of gender dysphoria arrived at a model based on precisely this notion: "Our hypothesis is that the individual who feels their body or sex is wrong is

[a] 1Pe 5:8–9, Jam 4:7.

likely to be defending against psychological traumas from the past."[8] Hatred of one's body usually arises from some experience that fuels self-loathing. Carefully revisiting the trauma, which can arise from different experiences,[9] allowing the Holy Spirit to redefine it in Christ, will put the person on a different path. Other factors, such as a fear of measuring up in one's gender, or a loss of vision for one's gender, are explored in the pages that follow but, in any event, the teen needs additional help to reconcile with his body and appreciate his gender, to see it as the beautiful gift that God sees.

D) Activism

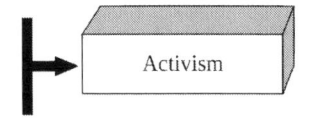

```
├──▶ [ Activism ]
```

There is another box that should be in your mind, as you are sitting there at the kitchen table. It is possible, when a teen, or any person really, says, "I am trans," the word signifies a passion to stand up for a particular ideology. They are convinced that the gender binary (God making people as only men and women) is harmful to uphold or even to believe in. People in their late teens, especially ages eighteen to twenty-one, have a propensity to want to save the world. This is a good thing. They often *can* change the world and, if the cause is just, for the better. If the cause that has captured their heart is trans, they may not really be struggling with their bodies at all. Instead, they have taken on a mission to aid what they perceive as an oppressed group. And so, they have plunged themselves into an identity—to support a movement of redefinition. Using the puzzle pieces that follow, you can help them think through more carefully how to actually help society and those they care about.

E) Adult Cross-Dressing for Arousal

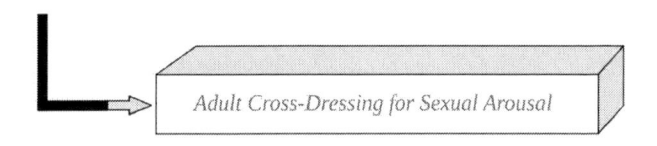

→ Adult Cross-Dressing for Sexual Arousal

One more box should be on our flowchart. It may not be what a parent is encountering in a teen, but I include it for the sake of completeness. In my experience, many adult men who cross-dress, sometimes in secret, do it for sexual arousal. Autogynephiles, as they are sometimes called, get aroused by the idea of themselves dressed as women. This exclusively male group is not brought up in polite conversation, but it is big.[10]

Once at a conference a young woman approached me and said, "My grown-up trans friend does not seem to have gender dysphoria."

I said, "Then I know why he is trans."

She said, "Well, I asked him why he cross-dresses. He said, 'For fun.'"

I said, "Do you want to know what the 'fun' is? It is sexual arousal."

She said, "Yeah, that makes sense, because he is often

making sexual innuendo jokes."

I have learned to expect this. These cross-dressers may or may not desire to live as the opposite gender. But that does not mean it is not a gender problem. It is another of the many ways we can use God's good gift of covenant lovemaking in the wrong direction.

These five boxes are what may be confronting us across the table. Diverse, are they not? But all under one word. We are now ready to assemble our diagnostic flowchart pictured on the next page.

This broad chart leaves out many details.[11] But it is a framework to assist your exploration of what the word trans means to a teen, and thereby, how to help him or her. The sizes of the boxes reflect the relative frequency of occurrence in my experience. It is difficult to get an actual count for each box as their relative sizes keep changing. So, take the bulk of a box as a suggested starting place. For example, these days, in a teenager, you are commonly dealing with a social contagion. The number of activists we encounter will be fewer.

The Kitchen Table Trans Diagnostic Flowchart

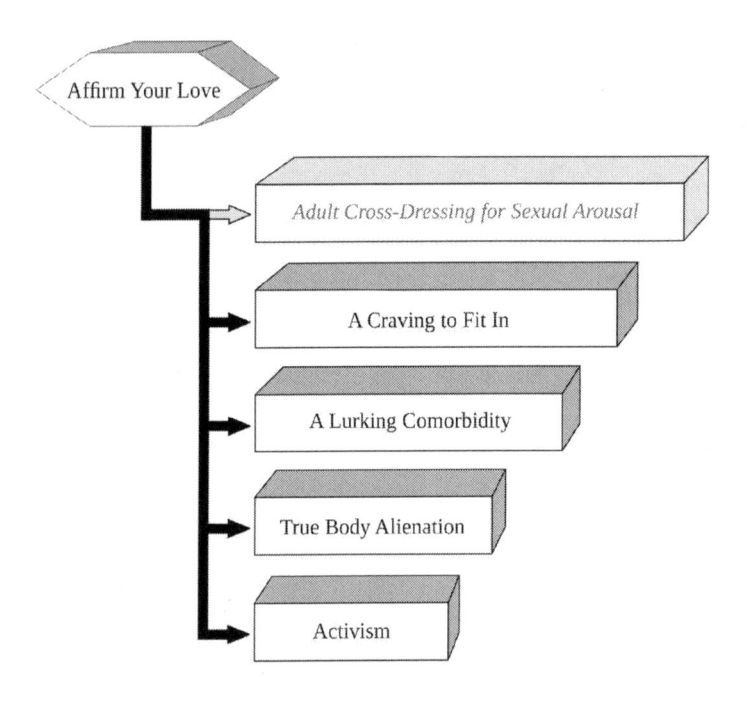

- Affirm Your Love
  - Adult Cross-Dressing for Sexual Arousal
  - A Craving to Fit In
  - A Lurking Comorbidity
  - True Body Alienation
  - Activism

People can also be in more than one box. They could have one foot in Body Alienation and another in Activism. A 2022 *Frontiers in Psychiatry* study of 3,100 Canadian students notes that the transgender youth in their cohort were the group at highest risk of supporting violent radicalization.[12] Certainly, a person otherwise troubled may have a strong sense of justice and misguided ideas about how to pursue it. Alternatively, addressing a person's co-occurring condition does not mean that you won't also have to clarify gender for him. Fred, one man I have met with, experienced multiple instances of sexual abuse as a child. Consequently, he cross-dressed for a seven-year period, into his teenage years. For Fred, the cross-dressing involved sexual arousal, but it was more a matter, as he described it, of being released from the pressure of being a man. Two boxes.

Any of these categories of trans presents a danger of serious damage. For all the boxes, the Bible's principles of gender can help us with answers around which to focus discussion. Scripture's guiding truths helped Fred, giving him a way forward to masculinity without hormones or knives. Today he leads a successful Christian ministry, very much a man and very much reconciled to his body. "Detransitioners," that is those who after living as the other gender now have reclaimed their own, will tell you that they used to be one hundred percent sure that they were trans. Until they weren't.

We proceed with truth and love. Truth without love is not very truthful. At the same time, it is not at all loving to withhold truth from someone.

BODY

*"Then the L*ord *formed the man of dust from the ground . . ."*

2

An Old Experience, A New Term

Trans at Ancient Uruk

At a recent conference I spoke at, a young person asked me: "If terms for non-binary gender or the transgender experience did not exist at the time writers wrote Scripture, how do we know non-binary does not exist and is not legitimate?" I appreciated the question's intent. Did the biblical writers even have the categories to understand the feelings and experiences of people who feel they do not fit as man or woman? Or those who think that they should be different than what their bodies are? Shouldn't we be sensitive to issues that the biblical writers didn't know about and thus couldn't be expected to address?

But the question assumes something quite wrong, namely that the trans phenomenon is something new to history. Pagans have rejected the gender binary from ancient times. Deuteronomy 22:5, which hails from the second millennium BC, forbids the Israelites to cross-dress: "A woman shall not wear a man's garment, nor shall a man put on a woman's cloak. . ." You have to wonder, if the prohibition is there, doesn't that mean the practice is there also? Why would they be so tempted if the experience were not part of their world? The apostle Paul, in the first century AD in fact, describes the breakdown of intergendered relationships and the accompanying dishonoring of the human body that attends any society that stops thanking God.[a] Apparently, even in his time, the apostle observed the breakdown of gender as part of a regular historical cycle.

In fact, we witness transgenderism much earlier, from the third millennium BC, in the cult of Inanna (known in Akkadian as Ishtar). Finding her home at the ancient city of Uruk (the hometown of Gilgamesh), Inanna was the goddess of transformation. In ancient Mesopotamia, the mind (located in the liver) had foundations and Inanna could overturn them. She was the goddess of [creating or ending] emotional distress, confusion, and turmoil. She also played with gender and sometimes dictated gender bending and blending in her worship. Some of her cult inscriptions speak of the "man-woman."

---

a Rom 1:21–32, esp. vv23–24.

An Old Experience, A New Term

Seal of Inanna, 2350-2150 BC [1]

In this impression from an ancient seal of Inanna, she's the one with wings and weapons coming out all over. Judging from what was written about her, this goddess was pretty good at mixing up womanliness with manhood, even in herself.

The most famous priestess of Inanna, a royal princess named Enheduanna, lived in nearby Ur and wrote prayers to the goddess. Sometimes hailed as the first published poet, Enheduanna wrote this prayer to Inanna in 2300 BC:

> Inanna was entrusted by Enlil and Ninlil with the capacity...
> To turn a man into a woman and a woman into a man,
> To change one into the other,
> To dress young women in clothes for men on their right side,
> To dress young men in clothes for women on their left side,
> To put spindles into the hands of [men...]
> And to give weapons to a woman.[2]

29

To these we could add other texts that attempt to blend or cross the genders in ancient Uruk. So, if you felt like you ought to be the other gender, you could appeal to Inanna to do the transition. Worshippers recited these hymns of her royal priestess over and over for hundreds of years. In fact, Enheduanna's influence lasted for a thousand years. Just because they didn't use the term "non-binary" or "trans-man," it doesn't mean that gender nonconformity, gender dysphoria, gender-crossing, gender-challenging, and gender-destruction were not part of their world. No, transgenderism has lived for a long time in the pagan experience. And the biblical writers well understood this.

Coming to Terms

But my conference questioner was correctly recognizing that our modern terms for trans, and its normalization, are new. From the mid-1800s, when this experience began to be described in medical literature, it was grouped with other deviancies as a sexual perversion. People who had it, and especially those who acted on it, were considered perverts. Around 1950, when the clinical-therapeutic view took over such things, as it was taking over everything else, that term was replaced by Gender Identity Disorder (GID), as in the American Psychiatric Association (APA)'s Diagnostic and Statistical Manual of Mental Disorders (DSM), Version III (1980). Though this new term discouraged condemnation of people for the feelings they had, which was good, it also vacuumed from the feelings any moral consideration. GID attaches no moral judgment to the experience, but also no moral responsibility either. It was a subtle shift away from the idea that God might have an opinion about such things.

An Old Experience, A New Term

Still, GID labeled the alienation as a psychopathology. It implied that there is something wrong with you on the inside if you have it. The APA, heavily influenced by the LGBTQ lobby, wanted to go further and made up a new term to remove any stigma from the condition. So, with the DSM-5 (2013), GID was changed to the enchanting term, gender dysphoria. When spoken, it wafts gently through the air. It rhymes soothingly with euphoria. It almost sounds peaceful. To those who experience it, it is anything but peaceful. But dysphoria has the advantage of being so clinical a term that ordinary people like us, who are not doctors and never use it in conversation, have no idea what it means.

Dysphoria simply means distress. Severe distress. Gender dysphoria means a deep distress with the way you are. The good part of this is how it helps more people talk about their feelings. If your teen is in the third box of our flowchart {Piece 1}, it can be intense and quite real. You cannot say to a guy with gender dysphoria: "Let's go have a beer and you'll get over it." Or to a girl: "Honey, you just need a dress that fits you better." But, again, the switch to the new term subtracted meaning in describing the situation.

The Right Man at the Right Time

You, as a parent, are the one to supply the missing meaning for your child. This book can direct you, but God has chosen you to be the real instrument of healing.[a] There is no one who can do it better than you—not a doctor, not a therapist, not even a pastor. I was recently praying with Ted, a father whose daughter, Theodora, started

a Eph 6:4, Col 3:21, Pro 4:1–4.

down the trans route, utterly ashamed of her body. This man helped her back at the time by affirming the truths we will be discussing in this book and what they meant for Theodora's body. We might picture Ted from this story to be a super-sensitive guy, a rare kind of man who can easily relate to a teenage daughter. But he wasn't. In our conversation, I heard a gruff, opinionated, and, he admitted, not all that sensitive guy. But Ted was her dad. And he loved her. If you talk to Theodora today, now married to a guy with whom she has had several children, she will tell you, "I don't know what would have happened to me if my dad hadn't been in my life back then."

In many cases of body alienation, you can be the help if you know that God's redemption extends to our bodies as well as to our souls.

3

Our Bodies Are Who We Are

Parts in Pictures

The first step to develop a Christian understanding of ourselves is to talk about what we are. How is a person to understand her body in biblical terms? The popular take these days is that our insides are who we are. Whether one calls it a soul, spirit, internal compass, or spark of humanity, the idea is that we access our true selves by what we happen to think and feel, out of sight of anyone else. Our bodies, then, are something of an accessory. The ancient Greeks had another way of saying this, with a pun that dates back into the haze of their history: "*Soma Saema*"! That means the body (*soma*) is a tomb (*saema*). Socrates responds to Callicles: "Once I . . . heard one of the wise men say that we are now dead and our bodies are our tombs. . ."[1] And the philosopher opines to Phaedrus of ". . .this thing we are carrying around now, which we call a body, locked in it like an oyster in its shell."[2]

Consider William Blake's conception, captured in an artist's etching[3] of Blake's drawing of the moment of death, made in 1808:

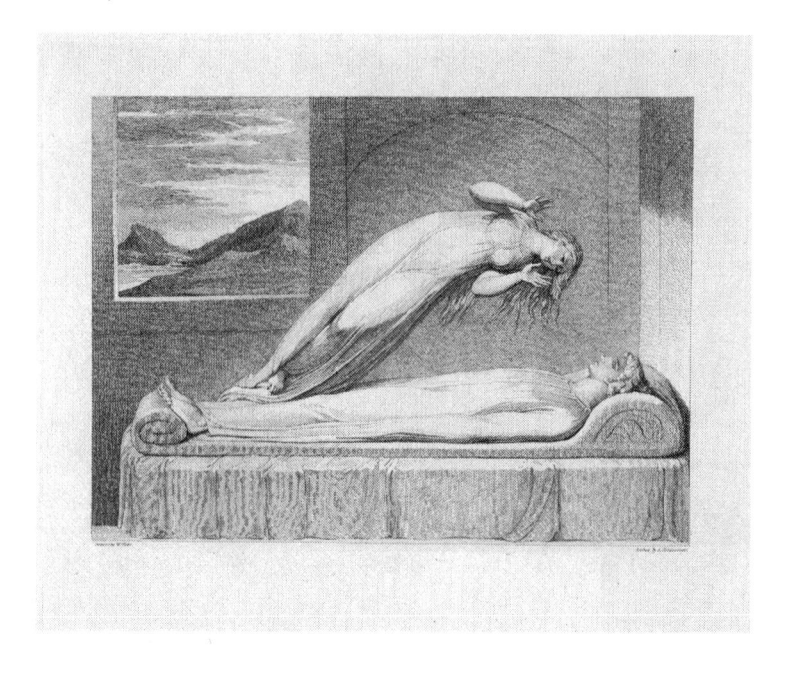

Blake pictures the soul, as it leaves the body, as the real, the true, the beautiful. In fact, our eyes are drawn to the soul above the body. It is literally the center of the picture. This centrality suits the sentiment of our day, in which the body is downplayed. The picture can serve as an allegory of today's dismissal. As prison or shell, the body can be modified, perhaps even should be modified, to suit our inner feelings. In the line attributed to Lili Elbe, one of the first men to undergo gender-imitative surgery, in the fantasy movie about the Danish painter: "God made me a woman. The doctor is helping by removing the mistake of my body."[4] It is like changing your iPhone skin.

The Bible presents us with a much different view of who we are. It positively exalts the human body. It is only when God breathes His breath of life into Adam's body that the man becomes a living soul.[a] Thus, it is not so much that we are "embodied souls" as we are more "ensouled bodies."

As Christians, we know that the body is integral to being human because Jesus Christ had to take on a body to become human.[5] He did not accomplish our redemption by floating around teaching and doing miracles. He assumed a body because it is a necessary part of us. This means that uploading my consciousness to a computer and having that remain "me" is, despite so many science fiction stories or the dreams of transhumanism, impossible. We cannot disregard the body in understanding our humanity or who we are.

Consider, then, a different "departure" than Blake's, rendered by another artist, a sculpture my wife particularly loves, depicting a person bursting from the tomb.

This sculpture is over the grave of the Polish Lewandowska family in the cemetery of Menton in the South of France.[6] The magnificent statue depicts the resurrection to come at the end of history. The top of the coffin has been pushed open and the person rises in full bodily form, exuding physical glory. It helps that the work is sitting outside on a mountainous slope. The exuberance is unforgettable. Here is the human body in corporeal celebration of our promised destiny.

a Gen 2:7.

The New Testament shouts out that because Jesus Christ rose bodily from the dead, we shall also.[a] That is, the resurrection of Christ proclaims the necessity of our identity in our bodies. The apostle Paul finds it impossible to conceive of our future life apart from our bodies.[b] The Bible's theology means that we very much *are* our bodies.

a Rom 8:11, 1Co 15:12–23, Col 1:18, Rev 1:5.
b 1Co 15:1–17, 48–54.

We could say, in the Christian view, the body makes visible and expresses the invisible soul.[7] The body expresses the person.

These are things to talk about with your teen. The question then becomes: What does this make of attempts to change ourselves by changing our bodies?

Did Jesus Understand Hair Dye?

Everyone turns to the Sermon on the Mount[a] for Jesus Christ's most sublime and important ethical teaching. But the part about not swearing oaths does not get much attention. That is too bad because it gives us important truth about ourselves. Jesus says not to swear by heaven, not to swear by earth, not to swear by Jerusalem. In fact, "...do not take an oath by your head, for you cannot make one hair white or black."[b]

Some may think that Jesus is a little dated in His teaching here. "Actually," you may politely murmur, "Jesus is quite wrong. I do exactly that every month, making white hairs black, as my hairdresser (and only my hairdresser) knows." We might be tempted to think, because of advanced hair product technology, that Jesus says many good things but on this point we've moved on: we can make a white hair black.

You might think this, I say, until you realize that hair dye was known and used in the ancient world. In fact, early patristic interpreters used this verse to say that women should not dye their hair. Consider the great Tertullian, writing *On the Apparel of Women,* in the second century AD:

a Mat 5–7.
b Mat 5:36.

> I see some women turn the color of their hair with saffron. They are ashamed even of their own nation, ashamed that their procreation did not assign them to Germany or Gaul: thus as it is, they transfer their hair thither...

After some talk about how the dye harms the scalp, he goes on:

> ...but, however, God says, "Which of you can make a white hair black or out of a black a white?" And so, they refute the Lord.[8]

We may question whether Tertullian should forbid dying hair on the basis of this verse, but his sermon shows that the ancients were quite aware of hair dye. That would include Jesus. So why would the Lord make this easily contradicted statement about changing hair color? As is always the case with Jesus' teaching, the closer one looks, the more one sees.

Dying hair turns out to be a perfect illustration of Christ's teaching, as your colorist also knows...and loves! He or she knows, once you've found the perfect balayage, you'll be back for more treatment. Because if you don't, your roots will start to show. Our continual hair growth means that, much as we try, we cannot really make a white hair black. We have limits on change to ourselves.

This is Jesus' point. You do not have control over many things (and so you have no right to swear by them), including what age you are or certain features of how God made you.

God has given you, in His love for you, certain strengths and limitations, which glorify Him as you live trusting in

Him. You might change some things, like fixing your teeth or getting in shape. However, you cannot change who God made you to be, no matter what the current technology, be it drug or surgery, promises. You cannot have the stature you may want, cannot stop yourself from getting old, cannot really change to be a permanent blonde.

And you cannot change your gender. You may cross-dress, take hormones, and sign a new name. You may even have a penectomy or phalloplasty. But you cannot change your God-given self by imitating the other gender. Rather, He gave you your body as a gift to tell you about yourself.

So our bodies are who we are. This insight, important as it is, does not alone address the discomfort a person may be experiencing. Let's look closer at the feelings—the very real ones—your teen may have.

Across the Kitchen Table

4

Where Our Dysphoria Comes From

True Confessions

To understand the meaning of these feelings, let's first listen to some of the most beautiful among us. A 2008 *Parade* magazine article commented on how amazing the actress, Penelope Cruz, looked in her recent movies. When the interviewer asked Cruz her secrets for looking beautiful, she replied, "I don't have any. I don't think I am beautiful. I can look good and I can look ugly."[1] Scarlett Johansson, after being crowned "Sexiest Woman Alive" by *Esquire* magazine in 2006, and again in 2013 (seven years later!), was interviewed by *Now* magazine about her appeal. She confessed, "I don't think of myself as sexy. I tend to see flaws in my appearance."[2] Keanu Reeves, dubbed "the Sexiest Actor Alive" by *Glamour* magazine in 2017 for a second year in a row, had this humorous assessment: "I am not handsome or sexy. Of course, it's not like I am hopeless."³

These quotes of movie stars are not hard to find. Your teen may have newer "idols" that she or he admires, and I encourage you to explore with them these kinds of confessions. They are clues that when you and I, just ordinary mortals, stand naked in front of the mirror, we are not alone in what we feel. Shame of the body runs deep within the human psyche itself.

All of us feel shame about our body, more or less acutely. For some, it never leaves their minds. Older folks who have lost the glow—and often the dimensions—of youth especially feel it. Those physically disabled or with bodies broken by accidents or ravaged by disease especially feel it. The anorexic feel it. And the truly gender dysphoric experience an exacerbation of this, our fundamental condition. They have been given a reason to look at their body in disgust.

We can hear the real issue when people who feel this acute disgust speak honestly about it. In the carefully constructed media portraits, we hear many statements about "feeling trapped in the wrong body." What is not allowed in the media creations, but is sung like a chorus over and over on transgender websites and in gender identity support groups, is this: "I can't stand my body."

Unable to Sustain the Gaze

As we noted in the introduction, the last we are told about the newly minted humanity before sin was this: "And the man and his wife were both naked and were not ashamed."[a] This is how the account of the world's beginning ends. The pristine experience of Adam and Eve

a Gen 2:25.

was of unencumbered nakedness. Imagine standing in front of a mirror naked and being unashamed. If even Penelope and Keanu cannot do it, it may be impossible for us to comprehend. But that used to be the normal human experience.

What happens next? Eve and then Adam partake of the fruit of the knowledge of good and evil and the sad fall of humanity ensues. What occurs immediately after the great sin recorded in Genesis 3? The very first thing they experience is shame about their bodies: "Then the eyes of both were opened, and they knew that they were naked. And they sewed fig leaves together and made themselves loincloths."[a] They fashion a cover-up of fig leaves and hide among the trees of their garden. God comes looking for Adam and when He finally finds him and asks why he was hiding, God receives the answer, "Because I was naked." In the story, that confession leads to God's query about eating the forbidden fruit.[b]

Consider the importance of this instantaneous transition. Before: naked and unashamed. After: naked and very ashamed. What happened to their appearance? *Nothing!* Nothing that we know of changed about the way their bodies looked. But how they looked at their bodies did.

What was it? The fruit they took was the knowledge of good and evil. With that bite, Adam and Eve took on themselves the role of deciding good and evil. That is, they became their own arbiters of morality.[4] They stepped into the place of defining for themselves what is the good, the true, and the beautiful—without God. To decide for one's *self* right from wrong, apart from God's evaluation

---

a Gen 3:7.
b Gen 3:10–11.

expressed in His revelation, is to put oneself in the place of God, a place one was never meant to be.

It changed the first couple's view of everything, including themselves. After they took this enormous step, they simply looked down. And for the first time and forever after, they saw their bodies apart from God, that is, apart from being in His image. Instead of this independence resulting in a feeling of freedom, the immediate and inescapable result was a profound shame. They saw their physical selves without reference to God, to being an icon of God, and it left them embarrassed and ashamed and unable to sustain the gaze.

Just You and Your Mirror

To experience freedom from *our* shame, we must first understand that it comes from the same step. We, Adam and Eve's children, have similarly put ourselves in the place of God, where we were never meant to be. So, as we look at our bodies, our value no longer comes from being made in His image, but from ourselves. This is what body shame is: looking at ourselves apart from God.

Sadly, we cannot see our selves, our bodies, rightly apart from God. Just you and your mirror do not tell you true. This is why the ways we try to be rid of this shame never work. Psyching ourselves up, dieting, or buying the right clothes cannot undo it. Even the beautiful movie stars, with near perfect bodies and unlimited spending accounts, cannot get rid of it. You and I cannot rid ourselves of our shame either.

This is what underlies the alienation from one's body. This is why teens, as their changing bodies draw focus, are particularly susceptible to the suggestion that they are in the wrong body. If they hate their body, it makes sense that trying on another body might rid them of the shame. Unfortunately, this is theological reasoning many people refuse to consider in trying to address gender dysphoria.

The story of Melanie and her daughter, from Kansas, is typical. Her daughter, Patty, had a difficult high school sophomore year, filled with panic attacks, depression, cutting and, according to her journal, suicidal thoughts {Piece 1, Box B}. Therapy helped and things calmed down. But Patty struggled with her weight and, through the suggestion of secular friends, at eighteen years old decided her gender was the problem. Melanie contacted me during the brief window when Patty was willing to consider alternate paths to address her distress. It took Patty five days to get an appointment with a gender therapist. In under than fifty minutes, the therapist diagnosed Patty (who then decided she was Peter) with gender dysphoria, recommended medical transition, and provided a list of physicians who could prescribe hormones and surgeons to do "reconstruction." Meanwhile, Melanie spent four weeks trying to find an alternative resource. Though she knew many Christian counselors, not one had experience with (or was willing to address) gender dysphoria. People in her church were supportive but unable to help. Hence, she ended up contacting my office, which is more than a stone's throw from Kansas.

For the gender dysphoric, the American medical establishment's current recommendations, as expressed in the canonical guide, *The Gender Affirmative Model: An Interdisciplinary Approach to Supporting Transgender and Gender Expansive Children* (2018),[5] is a path of binding, artificial hormone supplements and body dismemberment to help imitate features of the complementary gender. These are new attempts to be rid of the old shame that won't work. "There is no good evidence that 'transitioning' diminishes chances of suicide." That is not my judgment. Those are the recent words of the chair of the LGBT taskforce for the American Psychological Association (APA).[6] In fact, some careful longitudinal studies (meaning, conducted over decades) indicate just the opposite. The longitudinal part is important when evaluating these studies because it is only after seven or more years that the false hope the interventions promised is at last realized. One 2009 case control study reported in *Reproductive Surgery* found "Fifteen years after sex reassignment operation, quality of life is lower in the domains of general health, role limitation, physical limitation, and personal limitation."[7] A Stockholm study covering *every person* who underwent surgical sex "reassignment" in Sweden from 1973 to 2003 found a pronounced increase in eventual suicide for those who underwent such reassignment in the relatively accepting environment of that country. This was not a controlled study so we cannot compare the effect of not doing the surgeries. Yet, the study says, "Persons . . . after sex reassignment have considerably higher risks for mortality, suicidal behavior, and psychiatric morbidity than the general population."[8] More recent reviews reached a similar conclusion.[9]

Let me state this in simpler terms: our fig leaves don't cover what needs to be covered.

5

"How Long Has He Been Like This?"

Jesus the Diagnostician

A difficult case confronted Jesus as He came down from the mountain. His disciples had been trying to help a father whose boy was really messed up, but the problem was too difficult for them. What follows is the longest description of a healing/exorcism in the Gospels. The uncommon amount of detail affords us insight into how Jesus worked to restore people to wholeness. While we do not know all that Jesus did each time He made someone better, this lengthy example shows that it sometimes involved a process:

> When they came to the other disciples, they saw a large crowd around them and the teachers of the law arguing with them. As soon as all the people saw Jesus, they were overwhelmed with wonder

and ran to greet him.

"What are you arguing with them about?" he asked.

A man in the crowd answered, "Teacher, I brought you my son, who is possessed by a spirit that has robbed him of speech. Whenever it seizes him, it throws him to the ground. He foams at the mouth, gnashes his teeth and becomes rigid. I asked your disciples to drive out the spirit, but they could not."

"You unbelieving generation," Jesus replied, "how long shall I stay with you? How long shall I put up with you? Bring the boy to me."

So they brought him. When the spirit saw Jesus, it immediately threw the boy into a convulsion. He fell to the ground and rolled around, foaming at the mouth.

Jesus asked the boy's father, "How long has he been like this?"

"From childhood," he answered. "It has often thrown him into fire or water to kill him. But if you can do anything, take pity on us and help us."

"'If you can'?" said Jesus. "Everything is possible for one who believes."

Immediately the boy's father exclaimed, "I do believe; help me overcome my unbelief!"

When Jesus saw that a crowd was running to the scene, he rebuked the impure spirit. "You deaf and mute spirit," he said, "I command you, come out of him and never enter him again."

The spirit shrieked, convulsed him violently and came out. The boy looked so much like a corpse that many said, "He's dead." But Jesus took him by the hand and lifted him to his feet, and he stood up. After Jesus had gone indoors, his disciples asked

him privately, "Why couldn't we drive it out?"
He replied, "This kind can come out only by prayer."[a]

Let us trace Jesus' process. Addressing the child's need first turns into an instruction for the friends trying to help, in this case the disciples.[b] It then becomes an address of the father's need. Jesus talks to the father about the man's own heart as revealed by the situation.[c] We similarly find, in trying to help a condition like teen trans, God challenges our own hearts. As secular psychologists Susan and Marcus Evans recognize, "exploring the family dynamics is an essential part of any assessment [of gender dysphoria]."[1] As you help your son or daughter, God is after your growth as well. At the very least, a gender-troubled loved one will require you to grow in love and faith. Again, you, as the parent, are instrumental in your child's progress. Jesus works with families.

Then the Diagnostician turns to the boy himself. Jesus has a way of drawing the real problem out of people. In His presence, the evil possessing this man's son soon shows.[d] The boy is in the grip of a spirit that brings him to body mutilation. This self-destructive force has overcome his soul.[e] As Jesus observes the manifestation with the father, He asks the man a telling question about his son: "How long has he been like this?"[f] Jesus is interested in the history of the boy. It somehow helped to hear about what may have led to the present condition. There was something about its start, perhaps, to revisit.

---

a Mar 9:14–29, (NIV).
b Mar 9:14, vv18–19, vv28–29.
c Mar 9:22–24.
d Mar 9:20.
e Mar 9:18, v20. Mat 17:15's detail of the same story emphasizes the self-harm.
f Mar 9:21 (NIV).

Breakfast and Other Past Events

Revisiting the past, for a key moment when it all started, occurs in other places God counsels in the Bible. In fact, the first one. God revisits the beginning of Adam and Eve's problem by asking them what they had for breakfast.[a] He thereby takes them back to see the decision they made that has produced the shame under which they now labor. Isaiah the prophet conveys God's diagnosis of how Israel had, at one point, gone wrong in adopting another means of security instead of God Himself. He takes them back to a past key time when they somehow "made a covenant with death."[b]

So going backward sometimes helps people go forward. A probable cause of pronounced body alienation is earlier life trauma. As John Calvin put it, "Satan mixes up his attacks with natural means."[2] Sins by others against our bodies can greatly exacerbate the shame to which we are already susceptible. If one feels like one's body is the problem, a reasonable place to look for the source of that discomfiture is in an experience that would make one want to separate from the body. Unfortunately, childhood sexual abuse, an example of the kind of trauma that can derail a person's gender, can take place without anyone finding out until much later. It is worth taking a look at whether it is part of the story.

Sometimes, for example, in response to being hurt by a man, one finds in an abused girl a desire to be a man in order to not get hurt: "I want to be a man because men are not vulnerable." Early on, she makes a decision to never get hurt again, and this is the best way to ensure it. She deeply wants what she perceives as the protective

a Gen 3:11.
b Isa 28:14–19.

power of being a man. Sometimes, a sexually abused boy concludes, "I am treated by men as a woman, so I must be a woman." He internalizes his abuse and shields himself from the disgust by the strong desire to be a woman.

Two Questions

Walt Heyer is a de-transitioner. This is someone who has undergone chemicals and cuttings to imitate the opposite gender and then has come to regret it. Heyer has devoted his life to helping those who regret their sex-change efforts through his books and website, SexChangeRegret.com. In his website exchanges and counseling, he repeatedly hears the stories such as Trent's: "After nineteen years of living as a woman, I realized my desire to change genders came from deep-rooted childhood trauma, sexual trauma. . ."[3] Trauma as the potential cause of gender dysphoria is acknowledged in a widely used clinical reference text[4] but rarely pursued in practice. Rather, American therapists normally view the gender incongruence as the cause rather than the consequence. But Heyer told me that he has learned to ask the same two questions over and over: "When did you first feel this way?" and "Who told you that assuming the opposite gender would help?" These two questions often lead to a fruitful exchange in uncovering a historical event and a person's reaction to it that began the pathway to trans.

Of course, such a horrid experience as abuse as a child is very difficult to revisit. It is easier to just say, "I'm in the wrong body," and never have to speak of it again. But, if that is our reality, ignoring it further damages us. When a person is ready to talk about past excruciations, licensed counselors can help in providing the delicate care needed to make the recalling tolerable. Furthermore, revisiting such awful memories can only help if the person reinterprets them in light of God's presence and acceptance. As cited above, God directed His first "How long has it been like this?" question to Adam and Eve. God revisited their initial decision to help them connect their wrong reaction to temptation to what they were currently experiencing. He then lovingly clothed them, giving them a new way to deal with their shame.[a] Jesus' questioning of the boy's father showed that His presence can overcome any trauma, even if it dates to childhood.[b]

In Prison No Longer

When a greater evil has taken hold, as Jesus found in His diagnosis, God will take greater measures. One time, a cross-dressing man, we'll call him "Archie," contacted me at his wits' end. He came over from another part of the city to talk, and we reviewed his strange history. Since age fourteen, Archie had periodically adopted the persona of a woman. Therapist after therapist, psychologist after psychologist, told him that this is just how he was made. But it didn't help. He ended up in prison. When he got out, he said, "I am still in prison." He was, at times, close to suicide. When decades later he finally broke free of the addictive medications he was on, he began to have clarity about himself.

As he described his strange history to me and asked for my help, he made no bones about having a demonic possession. It was more a matter of Archie doing the diagnosing rather than me. He could tell that Satan lay

a Gen 3:21.
b Mar 9:21.

behind his man-denying behavior. It began with sexual molestation at six years old by an evil grandfather.

I do not tend to rush into these things. Archie had not been to church in twenty-five years. But he did understand his guilt and shame and need for reinterpretation in Christ. After further discussion, prayer and enacting appropriate safeguards, as I have done on rare occasions, I performed an exorcism. That was the beginning of Archie as a changed man. In my last contact with him, he wasn't in prison anymore. (We can expect more need for demonic deliverance as our culture continues its steady march to paganism.)

Trauma-induced gender tearing can be redeemed by re-understanding it to be inside the care of our heavenly Father and including it in the reason for Christ's work on our behalf {Piece 7}. But this the Holy Spirit is faithful to do with God's children. It is remarkable to see Him apply Jesus Christ's excruciation to areas of pain in our lives to bring about healing, forgiveness and, in the end, freedom. Yet this, He does.

Across the Kitchen Table

6

Sometimes We Are Wrong About Ourselves

Never Alone

Your friend may say to you, "I have a woman's body, but I am a man inside." Yet, how does she come to know herself inside? When you ask what she means by "feeling like a man," you get talk about gender stereotypes in response. One of the big linchpins of transgenderism is the assumption that we can know who we are without any help from the outside, such as from our bodies or our fuddy-duddy parents or our old friends or our Creator.

A moment's thought should undo the falsehood that we alone discover our true selves. Sometimes travelers in remote regions find feral children, who by accident were lost but somehow survived in the wild. These are people who truly define themselves alone, without any other person's expectations whatsoever. The result is horrifying. It is not like the romantic Mowgli story, "raised by wolves," in *The Jungle Book*. Actual feral children, deprived of human contact, incur permanent brain damage.[1] Even after rescue, these self-defined souls remain plagued by atrophy and asociality. They may learn to walk, but never run. They may learn to speak, but not with a vocabulary of more than fifty words. Why would this be? Because we are made in the image of the Triune God,[a] after whom we are named in families.[b] [2] When we are entirely alone, we cannot be human.

How do we know what our talents are? We determine them in the presence of others, by comparison with others. How do we find our true calling? We come to it in effective service to others. We need the many to understand the one. Our families or friends can sometimes be wrong about us. But we still need them to define our identities. The apostle Paul says that Christians are members of one body, that we are individually members one of another.[c] By that, he means that we are never alone. We never can determine ourselves alone, merely "by what is inside." We should not ignore what is inside, but we must interpret it with those who love us. And this is what we always do, even if we think that we are not doing it. So, whose interpretation are you listening to?

Earlier in my life, I decided to change my name. I was trying to remake myself apart from the definition of my family. It did not work. Oh, I got the people around me to cooperate by the way I introduced myself. I got the government to approve by issuing me a new birth

a Gen 1:26-27
b Eph 3:14–17.
c Rom 12:5, 1Co 12:27.

certificate. I also got a new social security card and learned to sign my name differently. The deal was done. But, late one night, I remember reaching a point of great alienation in my disconnection. I was looking in a mirror. I actually spoke the words out loud: "Who am I?" When I married, my wife helped me to see that I could not become who I was without my father's family. I needed to stay with them in heart, as distant as they were from me spiritually. They pulsed in my veins. There is no freedom from family sins without the forgiveness of them.

Besides family, we need our trusted and longtime friends.

Shall You Affirm Fatness?

If your friend is troubled about gender, a helpful question to explore is this: Can you accept that people sometimes, maybe even often, err in their self-perception? Take, for example, your friend's belief that she is fat. When your girlfriend is hanging with you in your bedroom and she blurts out that thing that has been bubbling inside of her for so long: "I'm so fat!", how do you respond? Do you affirm her inner feeling? Do you immediately agree because friends always back the dreams of their friends? No! Of course not. You immediately respond with "No, you're not." Especially if it is not true that she is fat, you love your friend by contradicting her convictions about herself. You do this even if those convictions are deeply held. You talk about what you see as true. You start to worry if she begins acting like she is fat when she is not. You don't change what you believe about her. Because you are a true friend.

Johns Hopkins University opened the United States'

first transgender clinic at a medical center in the 1960s. Paul McHugh, while psychiatrist in chief there, compared gender dysphoria with anorexia nervosa: "Other kinds of disordered assumptions are held by those who suffer from anorexia and bulimia nervosa, where the assumption that departs from physical reality is the belief by the dangerously thin that they are overweight.... They become persuaded that seeking a drastic physical change will banish their psycho-social problems."[3] But, McHugh concluded, as he closed the gender clinic in 1979, they are wrong.

What changes if your girlfriend starts to believe that she is a guy? Is it loving for you to change what you believe? Or can you love her by telling her what you really think is true? Is it loving for you to change what you believe? Or does she need you, her friend, to tell her what you see?

Our gender is especially found in our service to others, because gender is a matter of relationship.[4] Maybe clearing that up {Pieces 10, 11} can help. That is why those who have been in our lives for a while have a better take on us than a glitter family. They usually know us better than someone online, even if he has a million X (formerly Twitter) followers or she has scored a successful YouTube subscription number. And the most important outside voice we need is our Creator's.

What Happens When People Meet God

The Bible is chock full of scenes of God telling people that they misunderstand themselves. When souls encounter the living God, He spends a lot of time challenging their deeply held convictions about who they are.

Gideon first meets the divine through an angel, who

comes and sits by him underneath a terebinth tree at Ophrah. Gideon is covertly threshing his family's wheat in a winepress, rather than doing it openly, to hide it from the Midianites.[a] These roving bands would regularly come around and take what they wanted.[b] Rather than confront them, Gideon is hiding. This is not exactly an exhibition of bravery. But the angel begins by addressing Gideon as "O mighty man of valor."[c] That is, the angel must first help Gideon to know that he is different from how he sees himself. Thus ensues an argument about who Gideon really is.[d] The angel essentially says, "I know that you see yourself as weak but you are actually a man of great might." Gideon takes a lot of convincing, in which God patiently engages, and it changes the course of the man's life.[e]

Similarly, when God calls the prophet, Jeremiah, the Lord finds a man who thinks that he does not know how to speak.[f] God specifically informs the reluctant prophet that He intentionally formed him in the womb to be the way He wanted him to be.[g] The Lord goes all the way back to the womb to preempt Jeremiah's thought that he was a birth defect. His problem does not arise from something wrong about his body—for God was there forming Jeremiah—but from his need to trust what God says about him. Jeremiah might not immediately feel what God says about him. He might not see how God's revealed plan is going to work for him. But no perceived obstacle will prevent it. The One with the prophet will

a Jdg 6:11.
b Jdg 6:1–6.
c Jdg 6:11–12.
d Jdg 6:13–17.
e Heb 11:32–34.
f Jer 1:6.
g Jer 1:4–5.

Across the Kitchen Table

make it happen.[a] Jeremiah needs to trust Him to see how.

Likewise, when the angel Gabriel comes to Mary to tell her God's plan for her to give birth to Jesus, he makes sure to tell her first that she is highly favored. When Mary is troubled by this greeting, he repeats it.[b] Whatever Mary thinks of herself, she does not see how she could be a mother as things are. The angel gives her a vision for her future, assuring her that God is not limited by her experience of how things work.[c]

All of these exchanges involve people surprised by how God characterizes them in His love. They object with a kind of "But God, You don't understand my physical situation. . ." In response, God requires trust in His words. Many other characters go through similar identity reevaluations with Jesus, like the apostle Paul,[d] the chief tax collector, Zacchaeus,[e] and even the slave owner, Philemon.[f] Jesus (or in the last case, Paul) paints the future that He wants for His beloved one. That person, in response, must heed God's word where it contradicts his perceived identity and must recognize the latter as false.

God is still doing this today. George was a boy always more comfortable with girls, even adopting their mannerisms. After he was molested in middle school, he felt it confirmed his suspicions about having a feminine identity. His anxiety conditions always made that worse {Piece 1} so when, later in his twenties, he lost his job as a wardrobe stylist, he finally and firmly decided that he should become a woman. When George

a Jer 1:7–8.
b Luk 1:26–30.
c Luk 1:31–36.
d Act 26:9–18.
e Luk 19:1–9.
f Phm 1:1–25.

told me his story and was willing to pray with me, I knew that he was a man open to God's reevaluation. While the troubled man was visiting his parents who were praying hard for him, God confronted George in a way similar to Gideon or Jeremiah. George discerned the scriptural principle applied to him, as if God were saying to him: *This is not who you are. Who told you this is who you were?* George surrendered to God's redefinition of him. Today, he is the creative arts director in his church and is taking seminary classes. He struggles with some of the effects of his earlier decisions, feeling like he is now playing catch-up on life. But he considers himself worlds better off, having accepted God's evaluation of himself. He has been released to become a man.

Across the Kitchen Table

7

The Way Home

Consider how a trans friend of mine, renamed Alexandra, speaks about his experience:

> The way I describe it is by saying that when you look in the mirror and you see a face, you recognize it as your face. When you look at your arm, you recognize it as your arm. That wasn't true for me. When I looked in the mirror, it didn't look like my face. My body didn't look like my body. I didn't feel disconnected—I knew where all my limbs were and such—it just felt like I was living inside of a body that wasn't mine. . . . My brain was always trying to sort out a massive schism in its self-definition.

That is body alienation, well described. Could my friend ever be reconciled to who he is? It will depend on where he looks.

I often say the best thing we can do for anybody, especially those distressed about their gender, is to help

Across the Kitchen Table

them know God. He is our bountiful Creator,[a] our truest family,[b] our most truthful Friend.[c] The mystery of who we are depends upon our Redeemer. Long ago, John Calvin pointed out that you cannot know who you are without knowing God: "Without knowledge of God there is no knowledge of self."[1] In other words, God must be the starting point of our self-understanding {Piece 4}. If we try to know ourselves by just looking at ourselves, without knowing Him, we are guaranteed to err.

Let us know God by looking at His response to the body alienation of Adam and Eve in Genesis 3 {Piece 4}. In a surprising move, God makes a sacrifice to cloak the naked couple with something other than their shame. He takes and kills one of the precious animals He had created for them. He uses the skin of the animal to clothe them.[d]

The First Lesson

The first lesson from this for us is that we must turn to God for His provision for our shame. To be freed from it, we must acknowledge Him as God again. When we turn to Him, what we find is a similar surprise. God loves our bodies. He is not insensitive to our pathetic plight, nervously fashioning our fig leaves, unable to sustain the gaze of ourselves. When someone who matters loves your body, you are on the road to seeing it as beautiful. You become the gift that you are to yourself and to others. Corrie Ten Boom watched her own and others' bodies desecrated and degraded in a Nazi concentration camp. Afterwards, she grimly assessed, "Surely there is no more wretched

a Col 3:10.
b Eph 2:19.
c Joh 15:13–14.
d Gen 3:21.

sight than the human body unloved."[2] Indeed.

I was once counseling with Ralph, a gender dysphoric man, about his feelings about his body. I enjoyed getting to know this musically inclined, sensitive young man. As we spoke, he got more and more honest about the way he was looking at his body. In a particularly vulnerable moment, he simply held out his hands, palms down, and we looked together at the long, graceful fingers and wrists. "I hate these hands," he declared. "These are a girl's hands." I took his hands in mine and said, "No, Ralph, these are a man's hands . . . and you should take up piano." (I was thinking about how piano players would envy Ralph's dexterous reach on the keys.) This helped Ralph. The conversation was a step in turning back to God for His view on Ralph's body. The One who clothed Adam and Eve looks at your body in love, regardless of what is wrong with it or what you think is wrong with it.

The Second Lesson

The second lesson is that the first lesson was a promise of a greater lesson. Clothes for the first couple heralded the covering coming in our Lord Jesus Christ. What did Christ sacrifice for us? His body. And He did it in the way that would overcome our shame:

> And you, who once were alienated. . .he has now reconciled *in his body of flesh* by his death, in order to present you holy and blameless and above reproach before him. . .[a]

We have all kinds of alienation in our fallen state:

a Col 1:21–22, emphasis mine.

alienation from God, alienation from one another and, yes, alienation from our own bodies. But Christ's body was shamed for you, made utterly naked on the cross. Most portrayals of Christ's crucifixion leave on a loincloth for modesty, but those portrayals are inaccurate. Based on what we know of Roman crucifixion, Jesus was utterly naked.[3]

Not just naked, He was disfigured. Deformed. That is, He was made thoroughly disgusting to look at, "as one from whom men hide their faces."[a] Crucifixion was a torture designed to heap the most shame that could possibly be heaped upon a body.[4] Upstanding Roman citizens did not even want to think about it, much less see it. As the Roman statesman, Cicero, put it: "Even the mere word, 'cross,' must remain far not only from the lips of the citizens of Rome, but also from their thoughts, their eyes, their ears."[5] Why? Because it so shamed the body. During crucifixion's 200-year history, Rome used it to visually impress any potential rebels how much shame awaited them for misdeeds. The point was for whoever saw it to say, "I will never defy Rome."

Jesus Christ willingly accepted all that shame heaped upon Him. Because He was taking our body shame upon Himself. Where? "In His body of flesh." *Jesus Christ allowed His body to be mangled, so our alienated bodies could, once more, be beautiful.*

In His Body of Flesh

Stan had grown up poor but watched his parents care for other people's children even in their need. So, he and his wife, Maeve, committed to foster parenting in addition to

a Isa 53:1–12.

raising their two sons. Once they had been certified, they received one of these emergency phone calls for a placement. An eleven-year-old girl, Jean, had been institutionalized for her depression and self-harm. She was just released and needed a home. They said, "Sure."

"Oh, and by the way," said the caseworker, "he is trans."

"Uh . . . wait," Stan objected. "We don't have the experience for helping with that kind of person."

"Please!" begged the caseworker. "No one else will take 'him' because 'he' is trans." Stan stopped to pray. All he could think was that Jesus would not turn such a one away.

"Okay," he said, "we'll do it."

The couple adopted Jean's gender-neutral chosen name. Besides her troubled past, Jean had a number of other problems, like a difficulty with hygiene, which Stan and Maeve cheerfully accommodated. She couldn't shower because the sight of her healthy, naked body sent her into emotional spirals.

Little by little, as Jean experienced the love of a Christian household, she began to open up. Her other mental difficulties lessened. Her grades in school improved. After a few months, Stan began to realize that the state-appointed counselor was pressing Jean to take on a transgender identity as a male, demanding that Stan and Maeve get her a binder (for her chest) and insisting on visits to the LGBTQ center. The counselor also brought LGBTQ people into sessions with Jean without permission. When the counselor found out that Stan and Maeve were Christians, she reported them as bigoted, unfit parents, and threatened to remove Jean from their home.

Finally, on an appointment with an OBGYN for help with Jean's menstruation, Stan felt that they were not being straight with him about the medication she was about to receive. Jean was being ushered into a life track that would lock her into the denial of her gender. They halted the visit and left. On the long drive home, Stan spoke from his heart to Jean about Jesus Christ. He explained to her the gospel, that Jesus had given His body to be mangled for her. She was listening. That next Sunday in church she repented and believed in Christ.

At that point, Jean's gender dysphoria dissipated. Within a few weeks, she went full-on girl-ness, asking for (and getting, as Maeve was pleased to deliver) a completely new wardrobe of dresses and skirts, doing her hair, and writing in her journal about a crush she had on the boy who lived next door. These cultural signs pointed to a much deeper reality. The state-supplied workers were baffled that Jean was now a girl again, and that she did not want the visits to support a male identity, but they could not deny what she said she was. When, a year later, she was up for being placed with a family for adoption, she had one requirement: that they be Christian believers. Now into her teens, she remains a Christian believer and, I can tell you, very much a girl.

The apostle proclaimed that we who once were alienated, Jesus has now reconciled in His body of flesh by His death, in order to present us holy and blameless and above reproach before Him.[a] He wasn't kidding.

---

a Col 1:21–22.

BREATH

". . . and breathed into his nostrils the breath of life, and the man became a living creature."

Across the Kitchen Table

8

Desires Are Moral

All our desires have a moral direction. They are like those things we learn about in physics class called vectors. You remember. To call a vector what it is, you have to name its magnitude *and* its direction. As important as size is, you cannot just talk about how big it is (that's a scaler). No, then you get marked wrong. You have to specify its direction.

The same is true of our desires. They always take us in a certain direction. We can talk about how intense they are. That is important. Magnitude is part of the discussion. But we also have to talk about the way they are going. A child may desire to play with blocks (good). A child may also desire to avoid putting those blocks away (bad). A wife may desire to have relations with her husband (good). A man may desire to molest a child (bad). A teen may feel hunger (good). A teen may desire to cut herself (bad).

As we've noted, using the term gender dysphoria {Piece 2} removed harmful stigma from the experience. However, it also framed discussion of the condition without any reference to the morality of our desires. This is trying to turn a vector into a scaler.

James' Pregnancy Model of Temptation

Some claim that gender desires should be considered neutral. They are just there, and we ought not to judge them. The Bible's view is more nuanced. Take a look at how sin happens according to James, the New Testament writer:

> Let no one say when he is tempted, "I am being tempted by God," for God cannot be tempted with evil, and he himself tempts no one. But each person is tempted when he is lured and enticed by his own desire. Then desire when it has conceived gives birth to sin, and sin when it is fully grown brings forth death. Do not be deceived, my beloved brothers. Every good gift and every perfect gift is from above, coming down from the Father of lights, with whom there is no variation or shadow due to change.[a]

James' pregnancy model of temptation, if I may call it that, implies that our desires are part of the problem. There might be a long gestation period, a long time before we "show," but the trouble begins when we join ourselves to wrongfully directed desires. James offers this analysis to help us avoid the birth by preventing the moment of initial union with those desires.

Yet notice in that same quotation that James also affirms the goodness of what God has created. There are "good

a Jam 1:13–17.

gifts and perfect gifts." We should be sure to welcome them and embrace them. Desire for companionship is good. Desire for relief is good. Desire for marriage is good. Desire to know ourselves is good. These desires do not have to "lure and entice" us away but can direct us rightly. The direction must be judged by whether they align with God's will for us.

Thankfully, we all have many good desires from the Father of lights which we can celebrate. If we really want to find out who we are and avoid the path to death, we need to be honest about the desires we have. But then, we must also be honest to judge the direction of the desires. This allows us to disassociate our identity from desires that take us away from God's good gifts.

Nevertheless, you may say, "I have desires that I didn't ask for. They are unbidden desires." That word, "unbidden" is a little redundant. What desire ever arrives because we have asked for it? When is a desire ever an act of will? It seems like "will" and "desire" live in separate houses inside of us.[a] We still need to decide rightly about those unbidden desires. You ask, "How am I responsible for these desires that I did not choose?" You are responsible to call out the direction of your desires, just like a vector on a physics test. You are responsible to call those desires good or bad. As the ancient King Solomon put it, "Desire without knowledge is not good."[b] Is a desire taking us in the path leading to our flourishing (good) or in a way that goes against God's loving intention for us (bad)? We must name the direction. Otherwise, we get marked wrong. And life carries consequences that are much more serious than a physics test.

a Rom 7:15–23.
b Pro 19:2.

In my experience helping people with unwanted sexual attractions and cross-gender longings, I find that they need to disassociate themselves from these desires. They must do just what James' analysis advises, to *not* own them, *not* come into union with them, *not* become one flesh with them, *not* identify with them as part of themselves. "Uniting with" is just what a husband and wife do at the moment of impregnation. He is saying to her at that moment of James 1:15, "You are a part of who I am." That union with our wrongly directed desires, then, according to James, is the beginning of sin.

The Vector of Righteousness

So, James helps us to tease out the different elements of our experience of distress. The addict seeks comfort (good), but she may pursue that comfort through substances (bad). The angry man may have cause for anger from the injustice inflicted on him (good). His distress is not wrong, but a desire for vengence is (bad). If, instead, he refuses to speak or act in retaliation, he is refusing to bed with destruction (good). The depressed woman is not sinning in feeling depressed. But her desire to address her distress has a moral direction. To commit suicide, which is murder, is a wrong response to that distress (bad). If this woman seeks help, and sees the need to at times accept truths in spite of not feeling them, she is preventing the union of her desires with self-destruction (good).

Very often we have good desires turned in a bad direction. How do we judge our different desires? We do so by what God has revealed to us about "every good gift and perfect gift coming down from . . . the Father of lights." A jewel thief may relish the beauty of a fire opal (good). The impulse to steal that opal is mixed in (bad). God gave us sexual desire, which is a perfect present from the Father of lights, but it is now all out of whack in us. Sexual passion is very important in a marriage (good). The steamier the better. But it is destructive outside of marriage (bad). My sexual attraction for someone who is not my spouse is quite wrong. I do not have to have it just to be a man, as we often hear, and if I were entirely righteous in my day-to-day conduct, I would not have it. As the woman in Song of Solomon repeatedly says, "I adjure you, O daughters of Jerusalem, that you not stir up or awaken love until it pleases."[a] That is, these daughters shouldn't awaken good desires in the wrong direction.

To feel distress about gender puts you in that same morally vulnerable territory. Discomfort with one's body is not a sin. To feel distress is not wrong. It is important to be honest about it in order to understand our desire for relief. In the moments of interpretation of that desire, we are in James 1:14 territory. How we interpret our distress leads us to desire rightly or wrongly because desire has a moral direction.

How do you parse what you are feeling? It helps to recognize your body as one of the "good gifts and perfect presents," as discussed {Pieces 3 and 7}. From the other pieces of the puzzle, we can tell:

- Desire to be relieved of distress with your body (good).
- Desire to escape yourself by being the opposite gender or no gender (bad).
- Desire to help those who are bullied (good).
- Desire to contradict cultural gender stereotypes

[a] Sos 2:7, Sos 3:5, Sos 8:4.

(could be good or bad {Piece 9}).
- Desire to wear the clothing that imitates the complementary gender (bad).
- Desire to punish one's parents (bad).

Aiming the Arrow of the Child

Recognizing the direction of our desires, both good and bad, provides a way forward for us. Charles and Nora, already parents of two children, decided to serve God by adopting another. Although John entered their family as a toddler, he already seemed to carry a dark past. Among his other troubles, John couldn't stop fantasizing about being a girl. Their description is vivid:

> By the time he was four, he covered his head with yellow T-shirts and flicked his imaginary blond hair over his shoulder. His dreams, both sleeping and waking, featured him in sequined dresses dancing on stage, with no one in the audience knowing he was male. For years, he wanted to wear fingernail polish, dresses, high heels, and feather boas. His voice was high and his mannerisms were extremely feminine. He screamed his hatred for his body: "Why can't someone just cut 'it' off and put in a hole instead?" He fantasized about what he had never heard of: gender reassignment surgery. Our homeschool, all-male-except-mom family wasn't expecting this. We weren't expecting a son who kept sneaking into my dresser to try on my lingerie and became uncharacteristically calm when he wore it. We weren't expecting a son who wrote stories about himself dancing with a prince

at a ball. We weren't expecting self-portraits with long eyelashes and cleavage. We weren't expecting a son who took down his curtains to fashion an evening gown.

Their full story is an enlightening account of faithfulness and redemption, but I will summarize it here. When John's parents sought help for John as a seven-year-old boy, a Christian counseling group gave them the number of an organization that offered to do gender "reassignment" surgery. Instead, Charles and Nora desperately sought God for their son. They got sound advice about desires being moral and the importance of creating a vision for gender for John. They intentionally spoke of how Jesus Christ can cover our shame. With endless creativity, they compassionately addressed his fear of becoming a man.

They cried often. They bore much wrath. But, as they put it, God gave them eyes of faith to see their son. They caught glimpses of God's grace at work, and they celebrated them. Gender became a study for their family of six. The couple grew in their own genders and that growth became a joyful current for all of them. As John moved through his teenage years, he took more and more steps in masculinity. We all have to do this as men. It was harder for John. His life was not without struggle, but as an adult, he gratefully expressed to his parents, "I'm so glad you didn't turn me into a girl." He had gotten the vision and, now in his late thirties, carries that vision into his people-oriented job. John is a true man. His manhood began when he did not wed his initial, strong, trans-directed desires.

Affirming the wrongness of wrongly directed desires is

practically important for two reasons.

First, asserting the wrongness of gift-denying desires enables strugglers to eschew those desires. Whenever we do not want what He wants for us, it is an expression of our indwelling sin.[a] The Christian must be able to separate himself from desires to turn from them. We must be able to say, "These are not me. I experience them but they are not my identity. They are alien to my new nature in Christ." Adopting a label that identifies you with your desires because they are persistent is disastrous. You are finished even before you start.

Second, we affirm the wrongness of some desires to affirm the rightness of God's intention for us. It is important to name some desires as wrong to highlight the goodness of the rightly directed ones. To appreciate the beauty of our neighbor's house is good. To rejoice that our neighbor gets to have it is also good. To want it for ourselves, instead of rejoicing that our neighbor gets to enjoy it, is sin. It is called coveting. To name both helps clarify the joyful generosity of heart God wants for us and to celebrate the good He is creating in us. And when it comes to gender, we have a great deal of good to celebrate.

---

a Job 5:7, Rom 7:14–20.

9

Rediscovering Gender

Stuck in Limbo

Addressing shame can go a long way to helping a person come back from trans land. But even if that helps, we have only addressed half the problem. In addition to a person reassessing what she feels, she needs to appreciate what is good. If a girl despises womanliness, she cannot grow to be a woman. If a guy cannot celebrate manhood, he will remain stuck in limbo.

According to a 2022 Gallup poll,[1] one in twenty Gen X Americans (ages 43-58) now identify as LGBT+. That number is doubled among millennials (ages 27-42): one in ten. But it is quadrupled among Gen Z Americans (ages 11-26): *one in five* identify as LGBT+. This makes for 7.1 percent of all Americans, double what it was ten years before. It is likely higher now.

The numbers in the United States are matched abroad. Before it was shut down, the Gender Identity Development Service (GIDS) in the United Kingdom was the largest child and adolescent specialist gender service in the world.[2] The chart below shows the explosion in the number of GIDS referrals from 2009 to 2016:[3]

England's Rise in Gender Dysphoria Cases

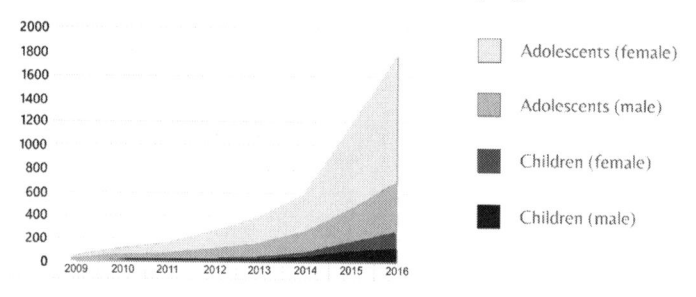

Number of Children and Adolescents Referred to the Gender Identity Development Service in the UK (2009-2016)

This graph stops at 2016. In 2022, the number of referrals to GIDS stood at over 3,500.[4] The graph's journal article invites comparison of England's numbers to other major clinics across Europe. The United States had just one pediatric gender clinic a decade ago. Now it has more than fifty.

Some suggest that these extraordinary numbers arise from simply increased awareness of the trans experience. Greater acceptance from society allows more to come out. But the size of the rise does not permit this explanation. The Bible suggests a more ready reason for this enormous spike: gender matters in relationship.[5] When the Scriptures bring up gender, that is always what the discussion is about: in relationship we find the meaning of our gender. If I am a man, I find out what it is to be a man first with other men and then in close fellowship with women. If I am a woman, I grow to know that with other women and then in fellowship with men. This means that when you lose gender in relationship, you lose gender. As a civilization minimizes gender in marriage and close relationships, its people lose a context to know themselves as men and women. They will then begin to ask, "What is a woman?" and "What is a man?" without an adequate answer. What comes next is, "What am I? How do I know I am a woman or a man?" Inevitably, more and more people in that culture will question their gender. This is another big piece of the trans puzzle.

Thus, in our time, you may have a teen who feels overwhelmed or repulsed by ideas like masculinity or femininity. Yet the Scriptures affirm the gender binary as a gift. The word *female* is used eighty-five times in the Bible. The large majority of these uses, eight out of ten,[6] appear with the word *male*, as in the beginning, emphasizing how the Divine Image comes in two flavors.[a] These good gifts have grown to a be a distasteful thing in the mind. Therefore, to help a person receive God's present of healthy relationship, we need to begin a positive construction project. And we should begin by admitting where our child is right.

Types in Stereo

Talk to your teens about cultural stereotypes. These are helpful discussions because we can agree with them and point out that the Bible does not endorse the stereotypes that hurt them and their friends. When people lose the Bible's message that gender concerns relationship, they always slip into sexism. So, yes, being a man does not

a Gen 1:27, Deu 4:16.

consist in lifting weights or scoring chicks or visiting the hardware store. Being a woman is not makeup or mauve purses or matching flowers. The Bible never says such things. Because none of these has meaning except in the context of relationship.

But don't stop there. Talk with your teens about the trans-celebrities they may admire so they can see that these cultural leaders engage in the same stereotyping the teens are seeking to escape. Elliot Page, neé Ellen Page, made a big deal about her move to live in imitation of a boy. Suffering from the typical comorbid conditions of depression and anxiety[7] {Piece 1}, and a failed lesbian union, Page made the announcement which immediately gave her a career boost. Becoming "one of the most famous out trans people in the world," she gained more than 400,000 followers on X (Twitter) in a single day. Likes and shares reached the millions.

Time Magazine's interview with the actress[8] opens with Page's feeling of triumph. What made her a man? She was allowed to cut her hair short. Then, at last, the actress declared, "I felt like a boy." Is this what is central to boyhood?

The majority of the article focuses on the need for political measures and for changing our close-minded society. But when it gets to Page's feelings, what actually makes her feel like a man consists in the surgical removal of her breasts and her wearing her hair short. The article ends:

> During our interview, Page keeps rearranging strands on his forehead. It took a long time for him to return to the barber's chair and ask to cut it short, but he got there. And how did that haircut

feel? Page tears up again, then smiles. "I just could not have enjoyed it more," he says.

Is this what it is to be a man, getting to wear one's hair short? Wearing a certain kind of clothing? If not, then what is it that constitutes manhood? The Bible helps us to transcend stereotypes, including those of the cultural idols.

Test Conversation: Boys Wearing Nail Polish

It is not uncommon now to see boys sporting painted nails. How will you respond when your son does? Or when his friend does? What's the conversation? You could react in a number of ways, such as...

#1 The Eruption Reaction:
What kind of foolishness is this? In my day, boys were boys and girls were girls! Now boys don't even know how to be boys! This new-fangled culture is emasculating guys and leaving them effeminate! And it is erasing womanly territory. Get some turpentine for those fingers. In fact, I have some right here!

#2 The Cool Reaction:
That's fun. I really like how you are a person with style who is staying up with the times. Of course, this says nothing about your gender, and I am glad you get that. Who said nail polish is just for girls? Good for you, breaking down stereotypes! You tell 'em, Charlie!

Do you tend to one of these reactions? The first reaction will lose a generation because it traffics in cultural stereotypes. The second breeds a church that will not stand before the culture in its current destruction of gender. But these are not our only choices. The Scriptures make a way for us as parents to neither freak out nor capitulate in our responsibility to guide. God may put us in these kinds of situations to sanctify us also. We then grow with the child. The puzzle pieces we have assembled offer another response, based on a more real view of what may be going on, which I want to call...

#3 The Christian Reaction:
This is worth a conversation: Male nail-painting is a new trend that means different things for the people doing it. I'd really like to hear your thoughts about your presentation of yourself and your service to others with this move. What does it mean?

Nails and clothing are always about our presentation of ourselves. We craft an image to others when we dress and go out. Even kids with the "I don't care what I wear" look are saying something deliberate, aren't they? So, what are you saying with this look?

The Christian reaction (which I recommend) begins a conversation. Over time, perhaps in further walks and talks, here are the points that conversation allows you to explore.

Think about this with me. If you want to tear down cultural gender stereotypes, to prove that society's ideas about gender are wrong, that is a good thing. I can applaud that. So, then, what is a real man to you? How will you show us what being a man really is? If you are not sure, let's start exploring that together—because painting your nails is easy. Being a man is not.

If you are trying to tear down the very gender binary

itself, I have to ask—why is that a good thing? Have you thought about it? If you believe that God's creational gift of gender is oppressive, why do you think that? Do you understand what the Bible says being a man is? Is it the gift or the abuse of the gift that you object to? The Bible teaches us that gender distinction, as expressed in our bodies, is a precious gift for others. Can we talk about what the gift does and why God gave us gendered bodies?

Is your nail-painting a creative statement to some end? On the other hand, are you doing it just to fit in to your group? To make a different point? Maybe I can applaud what you are doing, because I agree that there is nothing magically feminine about nail polish. But every culture has clothing and body markers to distinguish the man and the woman. Our culture always gives us clothes for our gender. There are markers of gender in every culture, and rebelling against these is too small for a life cause. Not because they are in themselves masculine or feminine, but they help us to say that there is a distinction. You have to ask, with this choice, if you are playing into the wider cultural movement of erasing any and all distinctions between men and women. You are aware of that effort, aren't you? What do you think of it? How can we stand against it personally?

Elisabeth Elliot put it this way:

> To do away with mere stereotypes because they have become useless or burdensome can be a healthy thing. But when, in the effort to get rid of them, we mistakenly attack what are really archetypes, we are in trouble. Promising to liberate and illuminate, we have lately limited and obscured the truth of our sexual nature.[9]

Furthermore, let's talk as Christians about how this serves others: our sisters and brothers, our friends. What does this move do for them? Nails and clothing always present an image, but that image should always be for the others God gave us to love. We have an effect on the people around us by what we wear. What is the effect here?

Nothing that we do with our bodies or what covers them is frivolous, because our bodies are us {Piece 3}. I am so glad your nails have started this conversation with me. Let's learn together.

10

Valuing Woman

Many teen girls who identify as trans today do not so much want to be men as to avoid being women. Others imagine that the masculine is just better. Both types need to reconceive femininity. There are many things to celebrate about womanhood, but this is where many of us as parents need to grow ourselves. A woman must feel the glory of being a woman, as the Holy Spirit through the Scriptures proclaims it to her, in order to pass on that glory to her daughter. A father must himself recognize the priceless gem of womanhood to convince his daughter of it. The struggle of feminine distinction is very old. Yet, when we see God's attitude toward us in Christ, we can overcome that struggle.

A Tale of Two Women

At a certain point in the synoptic Gospels (Matthew, Mark, and Luke), the authors bring together two amazing healings that Jesus did: the healing of a woman with an intractable bodily ailment and the raising of a young girl who died. Sometimes the different Gospels record stories in different settings, and leave us to figure out in what order things occurred. We ask, Is this writer trying to be chronological? Is he making a different point by his placement? And so on. But here, the order is invariable: all three writers want us to know that the woman's healing interrupts Jesus' journey to the girl.[a]

While on this trip to a girl on her deathbed, a *zabah*, that is, a woman with a bleeding illness, creeps up behind Jesus. She desperately reaches out to touch Him. Her desperation arises from the futile treatments to which she had been subject at the hand of doctors.[b] The prescribed treatments for a *zabah* at that time were indeed bizarre, like drinking a powder made of rubber, alum, and garden crocuses, or carrying around the ashes of an ostrich egg in a special cloth.[1] None of these, or others more expensive, had worked. (It makes one wonder how people in ages to come will think of some current treatment schemes.)

In any event, the story illustrates the difficulty of addressing the needs of this woman's body. I used to work at the New York University Women's Health Study, a research center where scientists studied various pressing ailments that women have. There I observed researchers often mystified by the health concerns of the female body. This temple of splendor houses many mysteries and, sadly, many things that can go wrong. Although these mysteries make for big challenges in women's health, they also, I thought, feature the glory of one destined to give life. One of woman's excellencies, her potential to be a mother, is also her liability.

Every young woman needs to see, in contradiction

---

a Mat 9:18–26, Mar 5:21–43, Luk 8:41–56.
b Mar 5:26.

to the idea that religion devalues women, that Jesus shows special sensitivity to women's concerns. Whether He is mourning the coming eschatological catastrophe for pregnant and nursing mothers,[a] or being moved by compassion to care for a widow in her grief,[b] or turning in His own agony of bearing His cross to comfort the wailing daughters of Jerusalem,[c] Jesus is all about attending to women as women. There is possibly even a suggestion in this story, when at the *zabah* woman's touch "power had gone out from" Jesus,[d] that Jesus knew, before He knew who had touched Him, that it was a woman's concern.[2]

In any event, this woman had a particular bodily need that Jesus could and would address. Afterwards, He brings the young girl back to life with the momentous utterance, "The child is not dead but sleeping."[e] Jesus had not seen her yet, so He was not offering a medical diagnosis. Rather Jesus implies that He is doing more for her than a resuscitation. The girl needed an awakening—a healing of an incurable body problem; a miracle of calling forth to awaken. God's providence brought these two signs together. They show us how Jesus Christ would use His amazing power for the mysterious matters of women.

Twelve Years

Mark and the other Gospel writers include what may at first seem like two insignificant details. How long had the *zabah* been afflicted with her blood condition? Twelve years. How old was the deceased girl? Twelve years.[f] The

a Mat 24:19, Mar 13:17.
b Luk 7:11–15.
c Luk 23:27–31.
d Mar 5:30.
e Mar 5:39.
f Mar 5:25, Mar 5:42

two details invite comparison between these two women. In fact, Luke puts these two mentions of the twelve years one right after other, in consecutive verses, inviting us to not miss the connection.[a] Why would this detail be so noteworthy?

Being twelve years old was very important to how ancient Jews understood women. The writings at that time of the Jewish Mishnah, and then the larger Talmud, give extensive discussion of a woman's early life stages, to determine when women were mature and able to marry and procreate. Age 1–10: she is a child. Age 11: she is underage. Age 12 to 12½ : a young daughter. Over 12½: an adult.[3]

The Bible celebrates, more than modern sensibilities permit, the glorious gift of bearing life. The older woman's complication in her body was her flow of blood. We cannot tell her age for sure, but this is a common perimenopausal problem, when the physical life-giving capacity is ending. That unique capability begins in a maturing girl with a flow of blood at about twelve years old.[4] The young girl's death cut her off, not only from life, but also from giving life. She is the New Testament parallel to the tragedy of Jephthah's daughter, who was cut off from childbearing to die as a virgin.[b] These tragedies we mourn in our world.

That is, until Jesus Christ shows up. He "awakens" this young girl at just the age to enter into her womanhood. This story shouts to us loud and clear that Jesus attends to women in the deep needs of their bodies. In providential succession, we see the Christ meet an older woman and heal her to stop her flow of blood. He then meets a girl and heals her to be able to have her flow of blood. He is

a Luk 8:42, Luk 8:43.
b Jdg 11:28–40.

there for women in every stage of their lives, to address them in their complex gift, to empower them, to say to them all, "Talitha koumi!"[a]

Bringing It Home

In light of this passage, can we let the women in our family know how Jesus Christ cares about their bodies' needs? He recognizes women as the beautifully complex givers of life. In the world in which we now live, the pain of a woman's body in its life-giving is greatly multiplied.[b] A lot has to go right. A lot can go wrong. There are many ways to be ashamed. While childbearing may be the farthest thing from our teen's mind, it is a concrete realization of the woman's call as life-bearer and life-giver. Can we celebrate that in the women in our household? What are the needs of our teen? Can Jesus be invited into the house to meet her in her phase of life?

There are many other feminine specialties to which you as a parent may introduce her, such as the challenge of loving a worthy man, the uniqueness of her prophetic voice, the power she has for mission, the call to bring rest in relationship. You are there to contradict her view of men derived from pornography, or from a culture shaped by pornography, which would drive any girl's heart away from wanting womanhood. You are the guide as so much changes in just a few years. She wakes up and the world is a different place. No longer is it all about drawing unicorns and solving math problems and practicing gymnastics, but more serious issues—issues of relationship, issues of responsibility, and issues of blood.

a Mar 5:41, "Little Girl, arise!"
b Gen 3:16.

Maybe the things happening in her body she does not like or understand, emotions that take her on a roller coaster. Maybe she is appalled at how guys look at her now. Or maybe she is devastated at how they do not. Let us note that Jesus understands. Just as He was concerned, even after the healing, that the now-healthy girl should get enough to eat,[a] He would make sure that you have what your body needs. And know that He is preparing you to be, in one way or another, a giver of life.

For anyone to be a true giver of life, she must receive the life of the Life-giver. That young girl rose to womanhood only because the power went out from the body that would bleed for her {Piece 7}. Maybe your teen has not felt His touch. Reach out with her to this One who has bled also to give life to us.

---

a Mar 5:43.

11

Beckoning Man

Hearing the Call

A man takes charge for others' benefit.[a] [1] He is made to be the ground (or *adam*) of the operation.[b] Boys need to be told that, to learn that, to envision themselves in that. This is because every boy begins in doubt about whether he is a man, or can be a man. Some boys need more telling than others, but all men start out like the prophet Samuel, awakened by God's voice from his childhood sleep, yet confused about it. The voice is calling this boy to take his place as the last judge of Israel. The work of God needs specifically a man to become the king-maker.[c] In contrast to the immature sons of Eli, the boy, Samuel, is to mature to be that man.[d] However, Samuel is not sure what he is hearing:

a 1Co 11:3, 1Ti 3:1–2.
b Gen 2:7, 15.
c At this time in history, God prepared the nation of Israel to enter into a covenant of kingship (1Sa 2:10, 2Sa 7).
d The narrator conspicuously interlaces the opening story of Samuel (1Sa 1:1-3, 1:25-28, 2:11, 2:18-21, 2:26, 3:1, 3:3-10, 3:15-21, 4:1) with Eli's sons (1Sa 1:3, 2:12-17, 2:22-25, 2:27-36, 3:2, 3:11-14, 4:4, 4:11) at Shiloh to contrast their degeneration with his maturation.

Now the boy Samuel was ministering to the LORD in the presence of Eli. And the word of the LORD was rare in those days; there was no frequent vision.

At that time Eli, whose eyesight had begun to grow dim so that he could not see, was lying down in his own place. The lamp of God had not yet gone out, and Samuel was lying down in the temple of the LORD, where the ark of God was.

Then the LORD called Samuel, and he said, "Here I am!" and ran to Eli and said, "Here I am, for you called me." But he said, "I did not call; lie down again." So he went and lay down.

And the LORD called again, "Samuel!" and Samuel arose and went to Eli and said, "Here I am, for you called me." But he said, "I did not call, my son; lie down again." Now Samuel did not yet know the LORD, and the word of the LORD had not yet been revealed to him.

And the LORD called Samuel again the third time. And he arose and went to Eli and said, "Here I am, for you called me." Then Eli perceived that the LORD was calling the boy. Therefore Eli said to Samuel, "Go, lie down, and if he calls you, you shall say, 'Speak, LORD, for your servant hears.'" So Samuel went and lay down in his place.

And the LORD came and stood, calling as at other times, "Samuel! Samuel!" And Samuel said, "Speak, for your servant hears."[a]

We can see in this story of Samuel's "grow[ing] both in stature and in favor with the LORD and also with man"[b] a

---

a 1Sa 3:1–10.
b 1Sa 2:26.

template of the maturing of a man. His uncertainty and misinterpretation are like every boy before he becomes a man, especially in times "when the word of the LORD is rare."[a]

Our boys are prone to mistakenly respond to the rumblings they sense by attending to lesser matters. Pursuits like video games can become the Eli's voice of their lives. They play to experience a sense of adventure, a taste of rescue, a semblance of heroism. But they misidentify the *Call of Duty* (a popular game) as the call, spending their time there instead of stepping into their life's quest. They respond to *Ragnarok: The God of War* rather than to the real God. A more serious lesser voice is the siren of pornography, which plays on the right desire for connection, a stirring of driving passion, meant to drive a boy toward responsibility, to propel him toward intergendered relationship, to do the things to become marriageable. Instead, the mistaken boy runs to sexual pleasure un-conjoined with the laying down of his life. Another mis-response is to give in to fear, like Gideon in the winepress {Piece 6}. Similarly in his response, Samuel runs away from the ark of God's presence to the familiar voice of Eli.[b]

But the most serious mistaken response is to give up hope that he can be a man. If a boy cannot see how his gifts fit into what he sees of manhood, he may give up the quest entirely. Being a girl might seem more doable. Thankfully, Eli also serves as the one to recognize the gift given to Samuel. He then properly redirects him back to the greater voice of the Lord.[c] If you are a parent of a boy, you similarly need to recognize his gifts and

a 1Sa 3:1.
b 1Sa 3:3.
c 1Sa 3:8–9.

help him hear the call to come forth.

Even when major problems do not plague your child, you, his parent, bring the Lord's beckoning to manhood. Even the king-to-be David, who seems as a boy to need no encouragement to take the reins,[a] still desperately needs confirmation that his life as a man is real. Key moments in his life beg for a hand on his shoulder, often supplied by his much older friend, Jonathan.[2] Valiant Jonathan aids David to visualize his future important work.[b] I have discipled many young guys. And I have come to see, again and again, that what they needed—and what my role simply was—was that hand on the shoulder to help them see that they could be men. Can you be the Eli, the Jonathan, the father, to tell the boy that he has more important things to do?

Swimming in an Alternate Universe

Looking at the award podium photograph of the recent national championship in women's 500-yard freestyle swimming, I was struck by the tragedy of what should have been. The National Collegiate Athletic Association (NCAA) followed the lead of the University of Pennsylvania (UPenn) policy and encouraged a boy who feels like a girl to act as if he was a girl, competing against girls and, not surprisingly, triumphing over them. NCAA and UPenn failed disastrously in their supervision by awarding him first place as a woman. The award ceremony picture is a sad illustration for the opposite of how gender should work:

---

a 1Sa 17:34–35, 1Sa 17:26.
b 1Sa 18:1–4, note with v5, 1Sa 19:7, 1Sa 20:1–42, 1Sa 23:16–18.

Lia (ne Will R.) Thomas, Emma Weyant, Erica Sullivan and Brooke Forde pose with their medals after the race.[3]

In an alternate universe, where the authorities addressed the disorder and gifting of swimmer, Lia Thomas, back when he was Will R. Thomas,[4] and did it lovingly and truthfully, I imagined a very different result. You have a guy who likes swimming and also likes the feminine. That is, if he really does identify with women, the disorder is a corruption of a sensitivity in him. Secondary sexual traits, like emotional intelligence and spatial thinking, are always overlapping distribution curves in men and women. Consider a trait eminently related to swimming: lung capacity. The chart below simply sketches the frequency of lung capacities in men and women of the same height. Men and women each vary in lung sizes among themselves, and that variation includes an overlap of sizes between the sexes:[5]

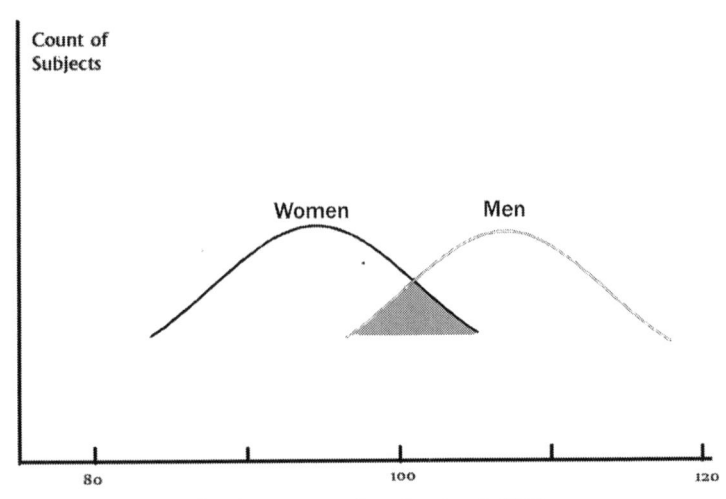

[Graph: Count of Subjects vs Total Lung Capacity (percentage of predicted male TLC), showing two overlapping bell curves labeled "Women" (centered near 95) and "Men" (centered near 107), with x-axis marks at 80, 100, 120. The overlap region between the curves is shaded.]

Total Lung Capacity (percentage of predicted male TLC)

The women range in lung volume from 83.3 to 105.8 percent of a predicted male lung capacity (TLC), with most women predictably falling in the middle of that range, around 95. The men range from 95.6 to 118.3, with most falling around the middle, 107. But this means that a few women will have a larger lung capacity than a few men, represented by the shaded region on the graph. God made this shaded overlap (95.7 to 105.8) with emotional and personality traits as well as physical traits. He did it so that people can more or less identify with the other gender. In other words, so we can talk to each other.

If some people fall within the overlap section of the curves on some trait, they can mistake that sympathy for identity. The ability to relate to women, even "identify" with women, is actually an uncommon gift in young guys. In Thomas' case it could have been well used. If UPenn, the NCAA, and the guardians who were raising Will properly addressed Will's disorder and encouraged Will's gifting, he could find his manhood in his assistance to the women in his life. The swimming community is something like a family, as sports teams usually are. Thomas' trajectory could well have led him into being a swim coach for women's teams. They would enjoy him and look up to him. They could trust in his decisions for their advancement.

I sat there imagining the big guy as a women's swim coach and how great that would be, a man making a way for the women he knows to thrive. Instead, in our world of loss, we see in the photo above a man grasping for his own glory, at the very expense of the close women in his life. He is boasting in his achievement against them while they must nervously acknowledge it. It is exactly opposite of manhood.

Platforming

As always, gender truth should lead us all, trans or not, to examination and repentance about our own relationships. Discuss with your teen how we are on Thomas' platform when we, as men, use our gifts and position to further our own ends at the expense of the women in our lives. Trans is what we men do when we do not take seriously taking charge for our family's benefit; when we do not counsel where the need is screaming; when we will not speak boldly to correct; when we do not pursue a worthy mission for God; when we do not secure what is unsteady. We become just like Thomas on the platform, confidently receiving a medal as if he had done something worth anything. The true women in the picture stand by, embarrassed and vulnerable.

A father's reimagining and locking of arms with your teen about his unique gifts, about your common call and even your failures, are what help a young man visualize his future as a man. We do not have to let UPenn's and the NCAA's massive failure in leadership silence the call to lay down our lives on the platforms we stand on. We can take up the call.

God gives man a uniqueness, and your encouragement can make him feel it: "You can be a man. You are a man. Take steps." Even if he has a hard time seeing it, there is hope. With man this is impossible, but with God all things are possible.[a]

The Man Child Comes Forth to Rule with a Rod of Iron

The New Testament commands gender distinction in relationship. Its vision of gender lies in calls of distinctive ways to love one another, those to which men as men are called to aspire.

> And a great sign appeared in heaven: a woman clothed with the sun, with the moon under her feet, and on her head a crown of twelve stars. She was pregnant and was crying out in birth pains and the agony of giving birth. And another sign appeared in heaven: behold, a great red dragon, with seven heads and ten horns, and on his heads seven diadems. His tail swept down a third of the stars of heaven and cast them to the earth. And the dragon stood before the woman who was about to give birth, so that when she bore her child he might devour it. She gave birth to a male child, one who is to rule all the nations with a rod of iron. . . . And the

[a] Mat 19:26.

great dragon was thrown down, that ancient serpent, who is called the devil and Satan, the deceiver of the whole world—he was thrown down to the earth, and his angels were thrown down with him. And I heard a loud voice in heaven, saying, "Now the salvation and the power and the kingdom of our God and the authority of his Christ have come. . ." [a]

In John's telling of the history of salvation in Revelation 12, he brings out the role gender plays in God's drama. He gives us the woman clothed with the sun who gives birth to the man child who will fight the dragon. Interpreters argue over different possibilities for the characters' identities, such as Eve and Seth, Israel and Moses, the church and the saints, or, of course, Mary and Jesus. Interpreters can argue about whom the passage represents because John is giving us the paradigm of salvation history. In each of those cases, it happens this way. Verse 5 gives us the boy that she bears who rises to shepherd and to rule. The child is presented as a *huion arsen*, "with the emphasis on his male sex,"[6] repeating an Old Testament prophecy.[b] We think of Christ, of course. But, in filling up the meaning of the paradigm, Christ is the masculine for us. Even losing His human father growing up, Christ became a man. Even deprived of that hand on His shoulder, He took the steps of manhood, answering the needs of His mother, recognizing and affirming His sisters in ministry, securing His "bride," the church, with His life. Man was born to vanquish the evil that comes against the woman.[c] He comes forth to make her secure.[d] To rule wisely and

a Rev 12:1–10
b Isa 66:7; Isa 7:14.
c Rev 12:5, 9–11.
d Mic 5:3–4.

well—that is, to take ironclad responsibility against evil.

That is what ruling means: to take responsibility, to preserve woman, to vanquish evil for woman to flourish. A man becomes a man, not when he benches 225, gets top score on a video game, or hits the home run. Those are great, but they are not where manhood is found. He is a man when he takes responsibility for others.

I have dealt with a number of big, hulking guys who insisted that they were really women inside. They will never really be able to pass for women, but they still sought to be non-binary or gender-fluid, just to challenge the categories. As I spoke with them, I perceived that they had one foot solidly in the Activists box {Piece 1}. In watching their grit determination and iron will in championing what they thought was a righteous cause, I would think of Revelation 12:5. Ironically, I could not help but admire their masculinity in taking a representative role. If, in the right moment, they could recognize and name this in themselves, they would be on the way to understanding the call of their manhood.

12

The Stutterer Orator

As a parent, a big piece to put in the puzzle of gender realization is a vision for your child's future in the face of ongoing struggle. The first thing for a struggler to know is that if a person is in Christ, God chose that person, in spite of the struggle. Our teen needs to know that God is not just tolerating him or her. It is not that he or she is one of the only ones God could get to hang around Him. God chose her. God wants him. The Lord has a plan about it. We all must learn how God works all things—that would be *all* things—together for good for those called to His purpose.[a] Here, then, is how to give a vision for the gender struggler.

What Kind of a God is This?

Have you ever noticed how God delights in turning someone's great weakness into his great strength?

God uses a man who cannot speak well, who was

---

a Rom 8:28.

"slow of speech and of tongue,"[a] to speak some of the most important words ever spoken. They were captured in something called the Pentateuch. This man, Moses, identified himself by his impediment. Yet this God appointed this man to a position requiring many moments of weighty oral communication, both to the Pharaoh whom God was challenging and to the Israelites whom God was delivering.[b] These roles demanded vocal leadership. Yet the prophet was speech impaired. What kind of a God is this? That is the way it is in His kingdom.

Gender dysphoric feelings are a disability in the sense that they keep us from acting confidently in the callings of life. Biblical characters often share weaknesses that have the same effect. All three matriarchs of the Jewish people were barren. In the Old Testament story of generating a people, the very children of Israel, God gave the patriarchs, Abraham, Isaac, and Jacob, wives who could not have children. Sarah could not bear children.[c] Rebecca could not bear children.[d] Rachel could not bear children.[e] All the while, God kept showing up, making promises to their husbands about descendants: "Oh, like the stars of the sky. . ."[f] "Oh, like the sands of the seashore..."[g] "Oh, a multitude of nations. . ."[h] God chose these women along with their signature weaknesses to accomplish it. There is a whole chapter describing how God brings specifically Rebekah together with Isaac.[i] God providentially arranged the marriages for them to

a Exo 4:10.
b Exo 4–19 tells much of the story.
c Gen 11:30.
d Gen 25:21.
e Gen 29:31.
f Gen 15:5, Gen 22:17, Gen 26:4.
g Gen 22:17, Gen 32:12.
h Gen 17:4, Gen 17:5, Gen 35:11.
i Gen 24.

play the leading roles in His story of procreation.

As Moses did with his speaking problem, these women over time must have identified themselves by this shame. It seems Sarah could look to her heritage from a noble family.[1] She could also cook. One time God and a couple angels showed up and Abraham rushed in, saying, "Quick! Prepare something to eat." And she fixed enough of a feast to feed a small symposium.[a] She was also pretty good at telling jokes.[b] But having babies, being a mother? "Nah. Not cut out for it." That was what Sarah saw when she looked at her reflection in a pool of water. She would say, "No I'm not that kind of woman." Maybe she even reflected at times, "I wonder if I am a real woman."

To makes things worse, two of their husbands weren't much help. Old Abe had a hard time believing how God would do this through Sarah. Or *why* God would do this.[c] Jacob dismissed his wife, Rachel, in her yearning rather than seeking God for her.[d] Lack of support likely intensified their identifying themselves by this inadequacy.

The Way of Faith

Gender difficulty is also a weakness that leaves one feeling intensely inadequate as a woman or a man. Just as Moses could have responded poorly to his weakness, leading to sin—refusing to speak, or the matriarchs could have responded poorly to their condition—refusing to engage in the actions with their husbands leading to motherhood, so the gender dysphoric may sin in

a Gen 18:6–8.
b Gen 18:12.
c Gen 17:15–19.
d Gen 30:1–2. Contrast Jacob with Isaac: Gen 25:21.

responding to their feelings of inadequacy by going in the opposite direction of their gender. But when they respond to the promise of God in faith instead, as Moses and the matriarchs did, God does amazing things.

Each one of the matriarchs became a mother, obviously.[a] It took years, but they underwent amazing reversals. In each case, because God had made certain promises, their lives conformed to those promises. Each of them was key to the fulfillment of God's covenant. These women became great women of history in their motherhood. They didn't just have children; they became famous for it.

How does God take our weaknesses and dysphorias and turn them into our strengths? The power for these true transitions comes from Jesus' resurrection. The death of Jesus was a greater shame and created more despair than any dysphoria we face {Piece 7}. But the resurrection contradicted that despair {Piece 3}. That event from the center of history guarantees conformity of the lives of God's people to the promises of God. That powerful reversal event sent ripples in time, reaching forward and backward in history, to effect resurrections of different sorts in the people of God. It reverses the destiny of the barren.

A Time to Heal

The fruit of faithfulness takes time to grow. Sometimes a long time. Like the vineyard owner in Jesus' parable, we may be impatient to see fruit in our loved ones or ourselves.[b] Yet the Scriptures should help us appreciate the

a Gen 21:1–7, Gen 25:21, Gen 30:22–25.
b Luk 13:6–9.

The Stutterer Orator

Holy Spirit's schedule. We should not let the intervals skipped in biblical narration make us miss the time God takes to do reversals. The process, for Rachel, was thirteen years.[a] Rebekah lived with her barrenness for twenty years from her wedding day.[b] For Sarah, living with her lack spanned many decades,[c] most of her life really.[d] It went beyond the point when it "ceased to be with Sarah after the manner of women."[e] She lost all reason to hope. Moses struggled with his identity for decades. The movie versions always want to picture Moses as a young handsome man, the movie star of the exodus. In fact, he began the Lord's speaking work at eighty years old.[f]

Ambrose was sixteen years old when he began living as a woman named Charlene. He rejected the faith of his mother, a Christian evangelist, to begin hormone treatment and laser hair removal. For eight years he paraded and advocated, being the most outspoken of all his friends for the right to assume one's own choice of gender. No one who knew Charlene ever expected him to identify differently. They also never suspected the truth: that during those eight years, questions gnawed at him deep inside, he hated himself, and he knew for certain that God was calling him to a different life. He heard the call but he did not know how to overcome his identity of shame.

It took those eight years for him to find out. Charlene

a The time between Gen:30:1–2 and vv20–25 can be seen in the intervening story. Jacob spent twenty years with Laban (Gen 31:38) minus the first seven working before he married Rachel (Gen 29:20). Then follows the time taken to build the family, enough time for Leah to have six sons (Gen 30:20). With the maids, ten sons had been born already before Rachel became pregnant with Joseph.
b Gen 25:20 and Gen 25:26. So there are twenty years between Gen 25:20 and Gen 25:21.
c Gen 17:17, Gen 21:5.
d Gen 11:30.
e Gen 18:11 (RSV).
f Exo 7:7.

happened upon a Wednesday night Bible study where participants were examining, of all things, the book of Revelation. Strangely, the alternate view of reality in the Bible's last book gave him hope that his reality was not as it seemed. After that, he met the lovely Marianne at the clinic where they both worked. She was kind and respectful, simply a caring friend, which brought Charlene's guard down. Marianne felt the movement of God—she also heard God's call for this friend. So, she gave him her number with the offer, "Call me anytime!"

The two were on an outing to Staten Island when Charlene finally confessed to her, "You know I'm a man."

"Oh, yeah, I know," Marianne said. His shock that she had known all along propelled a wave of honesty:

"I believe I am not what I think I am but I do not know how I could be different."

"Well, come to my church meeting," she smiled. And Charlene did. And the Lord changed Charlene back to Ambrose.

But heeding the call was only the beginning. The new, true identity only slowly could emerge from Ambrose's changed heart. It took some time before he could let go of the hair, and then the makeup, and finally the dress of Charlene. One morning, a year later, the nearby Salvation Army store got an amazing single donation in of unusually nice dresses, hats and handbags. (Whoever happened in to shop for clothes that day was in for a huge surprise!) It took a long time for Ambrose to understand and embrace the true identity God had given him. Nevertheless, his long-standing weakness is now his strength. He is so very happy now that God has made him a man. And so is his fiancé, Marianne.

Such accounts show that there is a gestation period to

these reversals of weakness. The conversation pointers in this book are only the beginning of many conversations and times of prayer that you may have. The feelings of dysphoria may take a long time to resolve. What is going on during that time? God is accomplishing the greater work of removing shame from the soul. He is taking the sore points, the wounds, and making them a cause to rejoice. An absolute healing. A real transitioning of shame into fame.

I've broken a number of bones in my body over the course of my life and I've learned what happens. When a bone is set properly and can heal, the area of the break becomes so built up it can no longer be a point of weakness. Thus, you can tell on the skeleton of a deceased person where the bones were broken and healed during a person's lifetime. It is virtually impossible to break a human bone in the same place twice. If there is stress on the bone, it won't ever fail there again. Similarly, God is taking those broken places in us and making them unbreakable.

BATTLE

"And a great sign appeared in heaven: a woman clothed with the sun. . . . She gave birth to a male child, one who is to rule all the nations with a rod of iron. . . . And the dragon and his angels fought back."

13

Psycho-Medical Science, History, and the History of the Science

Historical context is a critical discussion point for scared parents and troubled teens. Chronicling medical movements from the past brings perspective. Nowhere is that more true than in evaluating psycho-medical treatments.

Strange Science

In our time, we are witnessing in the West a strange relinquishing of scientific standards. Back in 2017, the Endocrine Society, an august organization representing about 17,000 members in the field of hormone research and publisher of the reputable journal, *Endocrinology*, issued a position statement on transgender health. They made this startling claim: "Considerable scientific evidence has emerged demonstrating a durable biological element underlying gender identity,"[1] that is, a gender opposite one's biology. I say, "startling" because it is so easily contradicted. According to researchers in the journal, *Clinical Child Psychology and Psychiatry*, numerous studies "unequivocally showed that the gender dysphoria remitted after puberty in the vast majority of children."[2] Averaging results of ten studies yields a figure of 85 percent of children claiming a gender identity opposite to their actual gender, if left to nature, growing out of it by adolescence.[3] Teen trans-influencers repeatedly stress the occurrence of change.[4] Furthermore, adults change their self-perceptions, transitioning and de-transitioning all the time. Evidence of "a *durable* biological element" would be baffling, front-page news and, if true, have sweeping implications for public policy and medical care. Hence, I carefully examined the two studies[5] cited to substantiate that claim.[6] It pays to summarize the research, even briefly, as the Society's conclusions give us a fascinating cultural artifact of culture-led science.

The first paper's authors' preconception about a fixed gender identity prevents them from thinking critically about the experiments supposedly showing a fixed gender identity. Their first section is on disorders of sexual development. The three studies cited seem to say the opposite of what the society claims: If someone has XY (= male) chromosomes, even with birth defects, many fewer problems are caused by raising them as boys. Over 25 percent of the raised-as-girls XY's went through the incredible effort to then switch to acknowledge their

Psycho-Medical Science, History, and the History of the Science

boyhood but none of the raised-as-boy XY's switched to girls. What does that say? Certainly not that there is this fixed thing called gender identity that is different from one's biological sex.

The second area highlighted neuroanatomy. The brain matter line of argument is based on a theory that transgenderism originates in a baby's brain development in the womb, since fetal sexual organs develop before sexual differentiation in the brain. The idea is that the brain could develop differently than the organs. What do post-mortem brains show? Gray matter studies of subcortical structures in male-to-female (MTF) transgender individuals show these brains to be "feminized," that is, more like a woman's gray matter. So . . . transgenderism shows up in the brain.

Besides the serious caveat that the studies cited are on a small number of MTF transgender brains, some of whom had done hormones or surgery, the approach confuses cause. The post-mortem brain studies cited are not proof of an inalienable or inherent, contrary-to-chromosome gender identity. Why? Because the remarkable human brain is plastic and changes through our lives. It has been demonstrated that changes in both white matter microstructure and gray matter can be induced by training or experience in healthy human adults. Just so, these transgender brains are certainly shaped, not only by female sex-change hormones,[7] but also by attitudes and behavior.

The authors even bear witness to this plasticity. "In speaking about what might be the cause of transgender feelings individuals have, researchers reported that sexual dimorphism in the BSTc [an area of the brain that differs between men and women] did not develop until adulthood."[8] Why talk of development of a brain pattern of transgenderism? Because our brains change, and we can change our brains. This explains the diverse data far better than the hypothesis of a fixed and unalterable biological gender identity.

One fascinating line of experiments tested smelling. Some compounds activate the hypothalamic networks in a sex-differentiated way. So, it was very clever (and fun, I'll bet) to compare the smelling ability of MTF trans folks to the sniffing of women. But even the two such studies that excluded hormone-treated transgender individuals, while valuable in showing the serious reality of gender dysphoria, only indicate association, not cause. Maybe the cortical thickness (CTh) was there originally, but it could also be there like a wagon wheel track deepened by reinforcement. Likewise, the white matter studies are ambiguous, unless you were looking for what you wanted to find. Some research found no difference in transgender folks. Later studies contradicted.

In general, with all this employment of brain studies to try to show an independent gender identity, the Endocrine Society falls into the Coexistence Vs. Cause fallacy. As one study cited sensibly puts it, we need further clarification on ". . .how disturbed gender identity affect[s] brain structure and functions."[9] In other words, it is not necessarily the other way around.

Finally, there is the evidence of Steroid Hormone Genetics. While wanting to claim that "select genes have been associated with transgender identity," the first study must later admit "studies to date on this topic . . . have been contradictory."[10] The other major study relied upon was much more responsible: "With respect to specific genes, association studies with transsexualism have been inconsistent and lacking strong statistical significance."[11] Like most claims to "have found the gene for X," this one turns out to be false. The remaining minor areas (Twin Case Studies, Neuroproteins, Prenatal Exposures) are similarly ambiguous. How does this show an "enduring biological element" to a contrary gender identity? Answer: It doesn't.

In short, the science does not really show what the Endocrine Society claims it shows, but rather something they want to see—justification for advocating cross-sex imitative procedures for the gender distressed. Rather than reflecting rigorous analysis, the Endocrine Society statement serves as a steely advance of another agenda. A recent revisit to that statement, six years later, finds the same two studies cited with no new evidence given.

This disconcerting surrender of standards by a guild is not limited to the Endocrine Society. One could present a similar analysis for the American Medical Association, the American College of Physicians, the American Academy of Pediatrics, or the American Psychological Association. It gives one a very disoriented feeling to see one's experts play this way with the data. And besides the data (or lack thereof), another avenue of investigation invites skepticism of the medical establishment's advocacy for certain kinds of "care": history.

Lest We Forget

Psychiatry is another field that is rushing headlong into severe procedures without evidence of either efficacy or safety. Mental-illness professionals, along with our federal government, now constantly assure us that the drastic pharmaceutical and surgical measures inflicted on even young people who are disturbed about their bodies are scientifically confirmed and clinically effective. Yet actual longitudinal studies on the measures are sorely lacking. Is this unwarranted confidence unusual? What has been the history of this field dedicated to treating some of the most vulnerable among us, that is, those with various dysphorias? It is a history we ought to review, lest the fog of the present prevail as it has in the past. This, sociologist Andrew Scull has done, chronicling the field of psychiatry in his 2022 book, *Desperate Remedies*,[12] called by the *Wall Street Journal* "an indisputable masterpiece." It is worth taking a page or two of our discussion to review a few highlights...

From 1870 to 1900, because of their unproven but confidently asserted theories, doctors of mental disorders believed they could cure mental disturbance in females by sexual surgery. For three decades, in the wondrous new field of gynecology, doctors performed what were called "normal ovariotomies," the removal of a woman's healthy ovaries to address various psychological and emotional disorders. Thousands of these ovariotomies were carried out across the US, and on a smaller scale in Europe. Many were done, in fact, in the neighboring town of my church, at the Norristown State Hospital of Pennsylvania. Patients were assured that this was a scientifically proven procedure.[13]

Sunshine and Sepsis

In 1909, California passed laws for the involuntary sterilization of those with psychological dysphorias. By 1921, the Sunshine State had done 2,000 of these sterilizations, 80 percent of all those done in the US. By the 1950s, the number done across the country reached over 23,000. Nazi Germany formulated their larger sterilization program only after carefully studying California's.[14]

Under the leadership of Henry Cotton, because of the theory that mental illness was caused by the poisoning of the brain by sepsis from other parts of the body, a movement arose to remove patients' tonsils and teeth. Beginning in 1916, the famous Trenton Asylum began these extractions and, with very shoddy science, claimed success. Soon this was followed by the removal of spleens, stomachs, colons, and cervixes, often bullying the patients and their families to carry out the procedures. These operations debilitated people for the rest of their lives, if they even lived. After Cotton's death, it came out that 44 percent of the thousands of Cotton's patients died from the removal of their colons. When, finally, a rigorous study showed these procedures had no beneficial effects whatsoever, that study was quickly suppressed by the institution and the most influential psychiatrists in the country. It was a business after all.[15]

After World War I, many psychiatrists were convinced by claims that injecting mental patients with malaria brought relief from mental trouble, and this treatment was carried on for several decades. We might expect that the medical establishment at large would never condone such a novelty. But instead, the doctor who pioneered this "treatment," Julius Wagner-Jauregg, was awarded the 1927 Nobel Prize in medicine for it.[16]

In the 1930s, psychiatrists published "scientific papers" claiming 88 percent of schizophrenic patients are cured by putting them in insulin-induced comas. Thousands of schizophrenic patients were brought to the brink of death under this pretense, destroying parts of their brains, to "treat" them. This procedure persisted for two whole decades, reaching its demise only when replaced by the first antipsychotic drugs.[17]

The Not So Olden Days

One might object, "Well, these things happened in the olden days. They just didn't know better then." But then, I neglect to mention the truly horrifying—and horrifyingly recent—history, when experts used frontal lobe lobotomies to "treat" various mental illnesses and depression. Psychiatrists drilled through a patient's skull and severed or removed part of their brain, doing permanent damage to offer mental relief, much like current penectomies and breast removals. While Scull, writing with typical British reserve, does not draw this connection in his book, the parallel with current recommendations for gender dysphoria has been suggested before.[18] The following statistics of the groundswell, for the United States, are most certainly undercounted:

1945: < 300 lobotomies
1946: > 600
1947: 1,200 or more
1948: 2,600 –3,000
1949: >5,000

These numbers show the trajectory. By the early 1950s, American psychiatrists and state hospitals embraced lobotomy as one of their best tools to cope with major mental illness. They performed it in greater numbers into the 1960s. Mental health institutions enthusiastically responded and promoters looked for ways to make what they called by the pleasant euphemism, psycho-surgery, more routine. Applying a local anesthetic, one leading proponent, Walter Freeman, began severing the brain tissue by thrusting an ice pick through the eye socket. He called these "trans-orbital lobotomies" and he performed them on children as young as four years old. As with others of these novelties, women were lobotomized twice as often as men. For this latter horror, again, its inventor, Egas Moniz, won the Nobel Prize. This was the preferred treatment just a few decades ago.[19]

Let's review. Measures that did little more than decimate healthy bodies become mainstream in dealing with dysphorias. Each wave of drugging or digging builds on anecdotes rather than rigorous studies. The techniques make their way to younger and younger ages, ostensibly to stop the mental illness before it starts. The innovations usually endure for several decades, until the harm being visited becomes impossible to deny. Chemicals and cuttings. Healthy body parts destroyed. Sterilization, either directly or indirectly, inflicted. And disproportionately visited on young women. Does any of this sound familiar?

Medical innovations are to be welcomed. And there are times to entrust ourselves to doctors—but not for novel measures based on faulty understandings and lacking real evidence. Not for the destruction of the body to allegedly help mental illness. As my wife succinctly summarized when surveying the field of transgender surgery, "Since when should we blindly trust a doctor with a knife and a new idea?"

Across the Kitchen Table

14

Battling Against the Body

Some people do not listen to me. Dysphoric inquirers I have sought to help with the principles in this book sometimes walk away from my counsel. They have set their hope on a conviction that identifying with their desires is the right way to go and changing their vocabulary, dress, and then bodies is the necessary path to relief. They are convinced that their deliverance lies in living like the complementary gender, at least as they suppose it to be. When that is the case, I need to let them go. But there is one point I ensure they understand before I do. The necessary discussion for anyone who considers chemicals and cuttings to imitate the complementary gender as a solution to body alienation is the personal cost of doing so.

Two Billion Dollars and Counting

As the following chart from Grand View Research, a financial investment service, shows, trans is a two-billion-dollar industry that promises to more than double in the next eight years.[1] As of this writing, puberty blockers go for $20,000/year. Testosterone treatments cost up to hundreds of dollars per month. Breast implants, double mastectomies, or vaginoplasties (false vagina efforts) start at $10,000. Metoidioplasty (the shaping of the clitoris into something that dangles and resembles a tiny penis) is $20,000. A phalloplasty, that gives a little more feeling, costs as much as $150,000.[2] For reshaping facial features, the sky is the limit. The progression of surgeries, addressing the complications that usually arise, and follow-ups, add up to big numbers. As Pedro, a transitioner who did not have coverage for his next surgery, put it, "It was either get the operation or put the down payment on a house. That was the choice."

Furthermore, for those who decide to live imitating the other gender, hormone treatments must continue for the rest of their lives. A man, for example, must sustain a regimen of anti-androgens to keep blocking his body from producing the male hormone while ingesting estrogen to mimic female effects. There are almost always additional medications, like progestin, that a trans person must take to address the continual damage that these cross-sex hormones cause, e.g., hyperkalemia, high blood pressure and blood clotting, heart problems, type 2 diabetes, as well as depression. A trans person is committing to a relationship to pharmacy and hospital for life.

U.S. Sex Reassignment Surgery Market
size, by gender transition, 2020 - 2030 (USD Billion)

$1.9B

11.2%
U.S. Market CAGR,
2022 - 2030

2020 2021 2022 2023 2024 2025 2026 2027 2028 2029 2030
● Male-to-Female ● Female-to-Male

Source: www.grandviewresearch.com

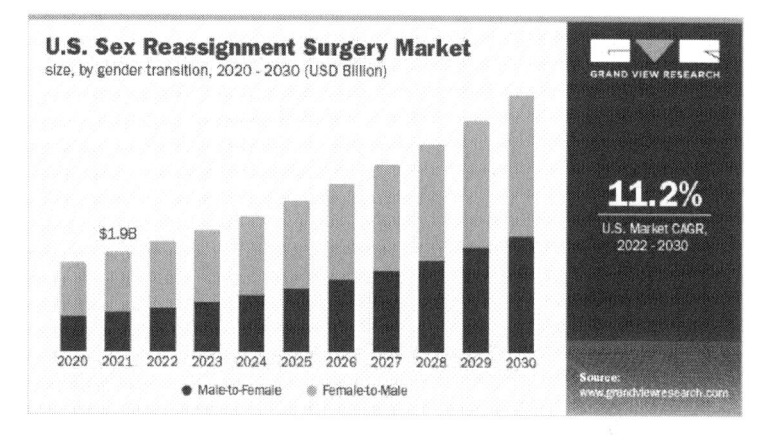

An Open Wound

In addition to the monetary costs, health costs are formidable. Their extent is unknown but will likely be quite steep. Even the beginning steps, such as chest binding, cost the body.[3] Relatively little research has been done on puberty blocking, but what has been published suggests destructive impact on bone density,[4] cognitive development,[5] and fertility.[6] That is why the drugs doctors use to suppress puberty (GnRH analogues) remain "off-label," which means that the FDA has not approved it as safe and effective. The list of increased health risks to women on a long-term program of testosterone is quite long.[7] And these are just the physical damages.

On Thanksgiving weekend, 2018, *The New York Times* published a brutally honest editorial by Andrea Long Chu, a thoughtful man who was about to have an operation to get a false vagina the next week. The essayist's point in this riveting piece is simple: he should be allowed to do this to himself if he wants. Long Chu has lived as if a woman for a long time, has researched the matter thoroughly, and entertains no illusions about the resolution he is choosing. The beautiful simplicity of Long Chu's writing makes the honesty about what is about to happen to his body all the more poignant:[8]

> I feel demonstrably worse since I started on hormones. One reason is that, absent the levees of the closet, years of repressed longing for the girlhood I never had have flooded my consciousness. I am a marshland of regret. Another reason is that I take estrogen—effectively, delayed-release sadness, a little aquamarine pill that more or less guarantees a good weep within six to eight hours.
>
> Like many of my trans friends, I've watched my dysphoria balloon since I began transition. I now feel very strongly about the length of my index fingers—enough that I will sometimes shyly unthread my hand from my girlfriend's as we walk down the street. When she tells me I'm beautiful, I resent it. I've been outside. I know what beautiful looks like. Don't patronize me.
>
> I was not suicidal before hormones. Now I often am.
>
> . . .The procedure will last around six hours, and I will be in recovery for at least three months. Until the day I die, my body will regard the vagina as a wound; as a result, it will require regular, painful attention to maintain. This is what I want, but there is no guarantee it will make me happier. In fact, I don't expect it to.

The prediction was borne out. A year after the operation left Long Chu even more miserable than he had expected.[9] This kind of truthfulness should give pause to anyone considering such a voluntary vaginoplasty or castration or double mastectomy. It also helps to view post-surgical pictures together on the Internet to show a person what it does to the body.

If this weren't enough, the trans person's immunity to disease is forever compromised. When Covid-19 hit a trans friend of mine, what might have been a passing illness for a healthy, thirty-year-old young man brought his body close to death. When I didn't hear from him for a while, I got worried. He finally was able to respond, "I keep getting sick and landing in the hospital for weeks at a time . . . I don't know when the last time I talked to you was, if it was around the stroke, or the numerous stomach bleeds, or the seizures . . . Covid has been very unconducive to me living my life."

These costs are so high because, in committing to imitation of the other sex, you are battling against every cell in your body.

6,500

Each of our 37 trillion cells is chromosomally male in a man's body or female in a woman's body. These cells constantly create differences that reach far beyond our genitals or visible secondary sexual characteristics.[10] In 2017, researchers at the Weizmann Institute identified 6,500 genes that are expressed differently in men and women.[11] These legions of genes, mostly active in one sex or the other, play a crucial role in our health. To attempt to contravene their action is to go to war against our bodies, which are, again, who we are {Piece 3}. So, in this war, the wounds we inflict are those for which we will pay, as Long Chu says, for the rest of our lives.

That is what I ensure the departing man or woman

bound for trans land understands. The great sadness is that there is One who took on those lesions for us {Piece 7}. The wounds we inflict on ourselves to cover our shame have already been borne by another. Can Jesus Christ's wounds be your answer instead?

15

A Message to the Church: The Last Shall Be First

Parents must help teens deal with the church. And help the church deal with teens. What no one must be allowed to do is devalue the person who struggles with her gender.

Honor for the Less Honorable Part

The Bible tells us:

> . . .the parts of the body that seem to be weaker are indispensable, and on those parts of the body that we think less honorable we bestow the greater honor, and our unpresentable parts are treated with greater modesty, which our more presentable parts do not require. But God has so composed the body, giving greater honor to the part that lacked

it, that there may be no division in the body, but that the members may have the same care for one another.[a]

How might we apply this passage? For years now, the church has possessed, and sometimes neglected, a precious resource in her midst: those who suffer from unwanted same-sex attraction and whom Christ has won to Himself. God has given these particular disciples important things to teach us as they repent and believe. I do not refer to those who champion such wayward desires and claim those desires as a blessing in themselves. These folks are no help to the cause of Christ because they identify themselves with desires God condemns {Piece 8}. No, I speak of those who themselves become messages written in their faithful living. For many years, I have walked with these same-sex attracted as they determined themselves differently in Christ. I have learned from their growth in going God's way, because, of all people, they understand the importance of gender in relationship. I have then tried to help the church see that these redeemed can help us appreciate gender in our own relationships.[1]

The church should be rolling out the red carpet for such overcomers. This doesn't mean requiring them to disclose their struggle any more than we require that of any of us. But it does mean creating an environment where their struggle is appreciated rather than vilified, where our preaching acknowledges this temptation among others common to men, and where we provide the support they need to align their desires with Christ in a culture that celebrates the opposite. Why? Because "God has so composed the body, giving greater honor to

[a] 1Co 12:22–25.

the part that lacked it."

Another Crossroads

We are now at another crossroads. The question of gender will more and more press itself upon the church. At the same time, society is about to be deluged with disfigured youth and adults. Over 150 colleges and universities in this country, including all those in the Ivy League, now cover gender-imitative hormones and surgeries as part of their Student Health Insurance plans.[2] In over half of the states in the US, Medicaid explicitly covers "transgender-related health care,"[3] which means that the dysphoric are encouraged to, and can attain, cross-gender hormones and sometimes surgery as medical care. As the Holy Spirit moves in people who come to the end of these measures and seek other solutions, many with trans pasts will be seeking out Christ in the church. What is the church going to do with these folks?

We can expect the same swirls to rush around us as have with cultural currents of the past. There will be a movement to celebrate transgenderism in the church, with hermeneutical gymnastics to accommodate the categories of modern psychology along with their errors. At the same time there will be the faithful, who have brought their struggle to Jesus Christ and are growing into their God-given genders. If we shut out those who have a trans past, we fail 1 Corinthians 12:24 miserably. The church loses out when she looks with suspicion or disdain on those who have gone in the way of the culture in the past but want to follow Christ. Rather God wants the church to live out His heart to "give the greater honor to the part that lacks it."

Forgiven Much

In fact, those overcomers with a trans past are invaluable to the church, worthy of a red carpet. Why? There is much for us still to learn about being created "in the image of God . . . male and female."[a] In this department, in what we could call our anthropology, we need improvement. The church must build upon her sound doctrine to more deeply understand what God has done in making women and men. How is that going to happen?

Who do you think, in the process of their redemption, will come to most deeply and viscerally understand the importance of gender? Our "dishonorable" parts, of course. Who will be able in this area to love much? The one forgiven much.[b] God is liable to make the gender dysphoric who trust in Christ to be the Moses and the Matriarchs of our time {Piece 12}. Recall, Moses resisted God's call before he finally surrendered to it.[c] Sarah sought other ways to relieve her suffering[d] before she finally trusted in God and followed His way (which meant, as an elderly woman, having relations with her husband). Similarly, decisions trans-people have made (or have had made for them) should not blind us to what God is doing in them now.

So, how might we roll out the red carpet for those we may know have a trans history and who come into our lives, wanting Christ? How might we do what we can to make them feel less shunned, less embarrassed, and more welcome? A big part is expecting God's work through them. Do you think God knew what He was doing in

a Gen 1:27, Gen 5:1–2.
b Luk 7:47.
c Exo 3:11–4:13.
d Gen 16:1–2.

sending Moses? Do you think He knows what He is doing now in sending the church these gender overcomers? Can we recognize the Spirit when He blows?

God chose what is foolish in the world to shame the wise; God chose what is weak in the world to shame the strong; God chose what is low and despised in the world, even things that are not, to bring to nothing things that are.[a]

He makes the last first. This is the way of His Kingdom.

---

a 1Co 1:27–28.

Across the Kitchen Table

Conclusion

James' S.A.T. Question

In the beginning, "the LORD God formed the man of dust from the ground and breathed into his nostrils the breath of life, and the man became a living creature."[a] The body and the breath make us living creatures {Piece 3}. As we've seen in our pieces of discussion, we must address both in their insoluble bond to address trans. We can see this same understanding of ourselves in the New Testament author, James.

The Body Is the Thing

In his letter to the churches on how to practically live out the Christian faith, James addresses more than the temptation to sin {Piece 8}. He takes up the perennial topic for people saved by faith: How do we understand the good works that we do? How do our actions of serving God

a Gen 2:7.

function in our salvation?[a] Perhaps correcting for an error of emphasizing faith to the point of making what we do unimportant, James writes that "faith without works is dead."[b] He then gives an explanation of how faith and works work, culminating in an analogy:

> For as the body apart from the spirit is dead,
> so also faith apart from works is dead.[c]

The analogy is like a question from a standardized test. The Standardized Aptitude Test (S.A.T.) used to ask this type of question to those applying to college. There are the vocabulary questions, reading comprehension questions, math questions, and then there used to be an annoying analogy section: Strawberry is to Kiwi as USA is to Canada? Mexico? China? None of the above? (These questions have since been discontinued, likely because they were so annoying.) James gives us his own S.A.T. question. His answer, however, is surprising. Greek, his language of writing, is precise. Like the standardized test, we need to read it carefully.

James does not say the spirit without the body, but the body without the spirit. He does not compare the spirit with faith and the body with works, as we would expect, maybe inside with inside, outside with outside. Instead, he pairs the spirit with works and the body with faith:

| As | body | without the spirit |
| So also | faith | without works |

What can he mean? For James, faith is the important

[a] Jam 2:14–26.
[b] Jam 2:17.
[c] Jam 2:26.

thing. Though he is arguing for the place of works, the thing that the works need to justify as alive is faith. Throughout his letter, James talks of faith as the essential: to be tested,[a] when asking anything from God,[b] as a corrective to partiality,[c] as the reward of those God has chosen.[d] James would not see works without any faith as worth anything at all, for he understands that faith is what saves us.[e] Faith is the focus. So too then, in James' mind, is the human body. The body is the important thing. James' analogy, along with the Christian emphasis {Piece 3}, can help us and our teen to see our bodies as our reality.

If we feel like our bodies are dead to us, that is because we have died {Piece 4}. Battling our bodies, then, will not make us alive. Chemicals and cuttings to imitate the opposite gender war against our selves {Piece 14}. Instead, our discussions have charted a different pathway to life. Allow Jesus to diagnose us {Piece 5}, accept His judgment about us over our own {Piece 6}, and receive His shaming death for ours {Piece 7}. This will make us alive like a living faith.

Making the Body What It Is

Furthermore, you cannot have one without the other. As James points out, the body, without the spirit, soon ceases to be. It decays, and is gone. So also, faith, not accompanied by works, ceases to be. If we read carefully, we can see that works that show faith are the works James is mainly concerned with.[f] Faith without trusting deeds

a Jam 1:3.
b Jam 1:6.
c Jam 2:1.
d Jam 2:5.
e Jam 2:14.
f Jam 2:21–25.

is like a body without the animating spirit. Deedless faith is dead. So, faith-filled works are the originating, invigorating, animating force behind faith. The deeds make the faith what it is.

So then, in James' analogy, the spirit makes the body what it is. There is a feminine animation invigorating your female body. There is a masculine origination behind your male body. The gendered spirit functions to make the body the gift to us it should be {Piece 9}.

Understanding this helps us attend to the originating spirit that makes our bodies what they are. We can interpret and direct our desires {Piece 8}. And we can do the gendered works that animate our masculinity {Piece 11} and our femininity {Piece 10}. Answering this call means that we are alive.

Why Is All This Happening?

Many Christians now feel buffeted by the Western culture in which we live. I am often asked why we see gender so rapidly disintegrating around us. In answer, I can point to how intellectual and sociological currents, flowing from the academy, weather and shape the culture. Some scholars of late have helpfully analyzed the ideological movements that render transgenderism plausible to society. These erudite offerings[1] demonstrate the deep and long historical tides of thinking that have made the gender identity idea make sense to people today. Decades ago, upon these philosophical undercurrents, the storm of modern gender destruction gathered in the laborious prose of gender theorists.[2] Those teachers sought to liberate people by demolishing the gender binary and what was called heteronormativity. Their teachings, carried along by generations of students, washed over the cultural landscape on which the Christian church is perched. I could also speak of the great red dragon, who always stands ready to devour the divine image. This enemy of our souls has with great delight stirred up the movement that whirls around us. Even the church herself has contributed, opening channels for this flood by minimizing gender in her midst. But none of these offers a complete explanation for the tempest now raging. For one Character rides this storm.

If a Christian feels clobbered by monstrous gender waves, it helps to recall the Bible's insistence that Jesus Christ is yet reigning over all.[a] And the Lord has a long history of using the societies around His people to drive them back to His Word when they need it.[b] Whether Assyria or Babylon or the newer empires-come-lately, He who rides the storm[c] employs cultural opposition to help His rebellious or hard-of-hearing people to reassess their direction or reform their application of the Scriptures. In our day, the Lord may use cultural waves to remodel His church, propelling her back to the Scriptures to more deeply understand gender, ourselves, and Him.

The Meaning Most Mysterious

And deep the Scriptures go. We are created "in the image of God . . . male and female."[d] Gender is the most mysterious feature revealing God's image in us. One of the blessings of the current cultural movement is how it mounts the meaning of man and woman under a microscope. The

a Eph 1:20–21, Phi 2:9, Col 2:10, 1Pe 3:22.
b E.g., Deu 32:21, Jdg 2:11–15, Jer 25:1–14, Amo 6:14.
c Psa 104:3, Isa 19:1, Job 30:22.
d Gen 1:27, Gen 5:1–2.

examination serves to expose faulty thinking. Do really believe that being a woman means nail painting, show tunes, and floral design? Is masculinity found in football and hunting deer? These might be things that many women or men like to do, but if some do not, the Bible helps us agree that they are not less gendered.

When God made us man and woman, and called it His image, it was not a decision arbitrary or defined by lower life forms. It was an expression of the mysterious plurality of God. All perfections are first in God, then in God's creatures. So both biblical authors, Moses and Paul, include the intergendered union of women and men as reflecting trinitarian truth about God.[3] Our knowledge of God from human relationship is not fully adequate for God. It is in every respect finite and limited, but not for that reason impure or untrue. We are poetry of God. So, Scripture pictures the Persons in the triune God for us in terms of different familial relationships like we experience,[a] including intergendered marriage.[b] In our world, gender is a key to how relationship happens.

This is why the gift of gender makes our relationships so intimate and fruitful.[4] Again, the apostle Paul's exposition on gendered behavior in marriage draws on Moses' "one flesh" account.[c] The "genderly" loved wife is like the husband's own body. They become one flesh.[d] Gender distinction enhances facets of intimacy as defined in sociological literature in dozens of ways: difference itself fosters interdependence; absence of competition fosters sharing; growth from interaction with the other builds identity; etc.[5] So, the Christian does not understand

a E.g., Eph 3:14–17.
b E.g., Pro 8:22–31, 1Co 11:3, 1Co 11:12.
c Gen 2:24.
d Eph 5:22–33.

gender as social norms ("Men like video games; women like romantic comedies."), nor as a collection of secondary sexual traits that often have an overlapping frequency distribution anyway ("Men are aggressive; women are emotional."). But rather, the Christian sees gender as a body-directed relational asymmetry among equals given to foster intimacy for themselves and fruitfulness in giving life to others. As such, gender is a gift to display God's glory. As we grow in gender with our teen, like Charles and Nora did {Piece 8}, as we explore the asymmetrical ways that the image bearers of God love each other, we know better the God who made us and we deepen our worship of the God who saved us.

I have been propositioned a few times in my life by men. One time, while I was walking in the woods, a guy appeared out of nowhere and told me to hop on his motorcycle. When I refused, he persisted. "Come on," he said, "there's nowhere else for you to go from here. This is the end of the line." That was supposed to convince me to comply. But I had seen enough good gendered life that it had the opposite effect. No, it was not the end of the line for me. I told him so and stomped off. Let us pray for our young people that the Holy Spirit will testify to the goodness of gender so that none of them have to make these gender-defeating choices, that none of them feel, "This is the end of the line for me." Instead, may they feel their engendered body in all its glory.

Across the Kitchen Table

Endnotes

Piece 1: A Trans Diagnostic Flowchart

1 Lisa Littman, "Rapid-onset gender dysphoria in adolescents and young adults: A study of parental reports," PLoS ONE 13:8 (2018):e0202330; Abigail Shrier, *Irreversible Damage* (Washington D.C.: Regenery Publishing, 2021). Dr. Littman invented the term for lack of any other clinical way to describe what she uncovered in her study of 256 parent reports. Ms. Shrier's book examines it in depth. A recent paper revisits the same subject through an even larger sample of reports of parents of young adults complaining of gender dysphoria: Suzanna Diaz, J. Michael Bailey, "Rapid Onset Gender Dysphoria: Parent Reports on 1655 Possible Cases," *Archives of Sexual Behavior* 52 (2023):1031–1043.

2 Annelou L. C. de Vries, et al., "Autism Spectrum Disorders in Gender Dysphoric Children and Adolescents," *Journal of Autism and Developmental Disorders* (2010) 40:930–936. The results reflected "considerable diversity" of sex, age of onset of Gender Identity Disorder, and persistence of cross-sex behavior. In other words, the connection between autism and gender dysphoria holds across the board.

3 E. Skagerberg, D. Di Ceglie, & P. Carmichael, "Brief Report: Autistic Features in Children and Adolescents with Gender Dysphoria," *Journal of Autism and Developmental Disorders* 45 (March 15, 2015): 2628–2632.

4 Joost à Campo, Henk Nijman, H. Merckelbach, Catharine Evers, "Psychiatric comorbidity of gender identity disorders: a survey among Dutch psychiatrists," *American Journal of Psychiatry*, July, 2003;160(7):1332-6.

5 Gunter Heylens et al., "Psychiatric characteristics in transsexual individuals: multicenter study in four European countries," *British Journal of Psychiatry*, January 2, 2018. Similarly, a 2005 study at Switzerland University Hospital found 71% of gender identity disorder patients had a current or lifetime Axis I diagnosis: U. Hepp, B. Kraemer, U. Schnyder, N. Miller, A. Delsignore, "Psychiatric comorbidity in gender identity disorder," *Journal of Psychosomatic Research*, March, 2005; 58(3):259-61. Again, ten years later, a similar result is given in Azadeh Mazaheri Meybodi, Ahmad Hajebi, and Atefeh Ghanbari Jolfaei, "Psychiatric Axis I Comorbidities among Patients with Gender Dysphoria," *Psychiatry Journal*, Volume 2014.

6 S.B. Levine, A. Solomon, "Meanings and political implications of 'psychopathology' in a gender identity clinic: a report of 10 cases," *Journal of Sex and Marital Therapy*, 2009; 35(1):40-57.

7 Kenneth Zucker is a professor of psychiatry and psychology at the University of Toronto. He was also editor of the journal: *Archives of Sexual Behavior*, chair of the American Psychiatric Association's Workgroup on Sexual and Gender Identity Disorders in 2007, psychologist-in-chief at Toronto's Center for Addiction and Mental Health (CAMH) and head of its Gender Identity Service. He oversaw the writing of DSM-5's definition of gender dysphoria in 2012, and co-wrote the "Standards of Care" for the World Professional Associate for Transgender Health in 2011. Helen Joyce, *Trans: When Ideology Meets Reality* (London: One-

world Publications, 2021), notes that Dr. Zucker "has assessed at least 1,500 gender-dysphoric children and adolescents" (p76). An examination of outcomes in hundreds of the cases he treated where the parents did not encourage imitation of the opposite gender found 88% resolved with their given body: Shrier, *Irreversible Damage*, 124.

8 Susan Evans and Marcus Evans, *Gender Dysphoria: A Therapeutic Model for Working with Children, Adolescents and Young Adults* (Oxfordshire, Oxford, England: Phoenix Publishing House Ltd., 2021), 3-7.

9 Adverse Children's Experiences (ACE's) which can cause trauma include sexual and physical abuse, of course, but also parents' divorce, drug addiction or incarceration, death of a close family member, or frequently moving.

10 Ray Blanchard, the Toronto psychologist who coined the term *autogynephilia* in the 1980s, observed it almost exclusively in men, though apparently extremely rarely in women: Joyce, *Trans*, 92. For a wholly sympathetic sociological treatment of autogynephilia, with many anecdotes, one may turn to J. Michael Bailey, *The Man Who Would Be Queen* (Washington D.C.: Joseph Henry Press, 2003).

11 There are many ways our sexual identities can be disordered. For example, therapist Andrew Rodriguez observes a few other boxes, that is trans categories, such as what could be called the "failed homosexual," who says "I cannot make it as a gay guy so I must be a woman," or the woman with same-sex attraction who tries to pass as a man to attract women.

12 Diana Miconi, et al., "Meaning in Life, Future Orientation and Support for Violent Radicalization Among Canadian College Students During the COVID-19 Pandemic," *Frontiers in Psychiatry* 13: 765908, February 11, 2022.

Piece 2: An Old Experience, A New Term

1 Image: Sailko, Wikimedia Commons
2 Anne Draffkorn Kilmer, "An Oration on Babylon," *Altorientalische Forschungen* 18:1 (1991), 16.

Piece 3: Our Bodies Are Who We Are

1 Plato, *Gorgias* 493a, *Plato: Complete Works* John M. Cooper editor (Indianapolis, IN: Hackett Publishing Company, 1997), 836.

2 Plato, *Phaedrus* 250c, ibid., 528.

3 I. Schiavonatti (Cadell & Davies, Strand, (5/01/1808)), [public domain].

4 Lucinda Coxon, *The Danish Girl*, Universal Pictures, 2015. The film, based on a novel, romanticizes and so distorts the sad history of Lili Elbe. In real life, Gerda, Lili's wife, a lesbian, and Lili practiced an open marriage. Lili died at the fifth operation, seeking to get a transplant of ovaries.

5 I thank Enoch Andreades for pointing this out to me.

6 Photo by Tangopaso, public domain, April 7, 2012. https://commons.wikimedia.org/wiki/File:Tombeau_Lewandowska_Menton.jpg

7 Pope John Paul II, of course, developed these ideas fully: John Paul II, *Man and Woman He Created Them, A Theology of the Body,* tr. Michael Waldstein (Boston: Pauline Books & Media, 2006), 206.

8 Tertullian, "On the Apparel of Women" II.6, in *Ante-Nicene Fathers. Translations of the Writings of the Fathers Down to A.D. 325*, ed. Alexander Roberts, James Donaldson, and A. Cleveland Coxe, 10 vols. (Peabody, MA: Hendrickson Publishers, 1995, orig. published 1885–96), IV:21.

Endnotes

Piece 4: Where Our Dysphoria Comes From

1 "Penelope Cruz: I Don't Think I'm Beautiful," *Parade* Magazine interview, August 8, 2008.
2 "Scarlett Johansson: I don't think I'm sexy" *CelebsNow, Now* Magazine, May 12, 2007.
3 Keanu Reeves, according to Brainy Quote webpage. https://www.brainyquote.com/authors/keanu-reeves-quotes
4 I draw here on Dr. Bruce Waltke's explanation of the tree of the knowledge of good and evil in Bruce K. Waltke, *Genesis: A Commentary* (Grand Rapids: Zondervan, 2001), 86: "'Good and evil' is a merism for all moral knowledge: the capacity to create a system of ethics and make moral judgments."
5 Colt Keo-Meier and Diane Ehrensaft, eds, *The Gender Affirmative Model: An Interdisciplinary Approach to Supporting Transgender and Gender Expansive Children* (American Psychological Association, 2018).
6 Mark A. Yarhouse, "Navigating Gender Identity Religious Identity Conflicts in Clinical Practice and Ministry," lecture delivered at ServingLeaders Ministries Seminar, Wayne, PA., April 08, 2022. Dr. Yarhouse promotes an approach in his books supporting gender imitative drugs and surgery (as explained in https://affirminggender.com/2023/04/07/no-fixed-outcome-except-for-one-review-of-when-children-come-out-a-guide-for-christian-parents-by-mark-yarhouse-and-olya-zaporozhets/). Yet even he must admit the ineffectiveness of such measures in curtailing suicide. Shrier, *Irreversible Damage*, 118, also cites a report from the Tavistock and Portman Trust gender clinic in the UK showing that the rates of self-harm and suicidality did not decrease after puberty suppression for adolescent girls.
7 A. Kuhn, C. Bodmer, W. Stadlmayr, P. Kuhn, Mueller, M. Birkhäuser, "Quality of life 15 years after sex reassignment surgery for transsexualism," *Fertility and Sterility* Volume 92, No 5 (Nov, 2009):1685-1689.e3.
8 C. Dhejne, P. Lichtenstein, M. Boman, A.L.V. Johansson, N. Langstrom, et al., "Long-Term Follow-Up of Transsexual Persons Undergoing Sex Reassignment Surgery: Cohort Study in Sweden." PLoS ONE 6(2): e16885 (2011). The study covered all procedures performed from 1973 to 2003. Interestingly, the increase of suicide was more pronounced when there was a longer period from the operation to the study's evaluation.
9 Paul W. Hruz, "Deficiencies in Scientific Evidence for Medical Management of Gender Dysphoria," *Linacre Quarterly* 87:1 (2020, Feb):38, in reviewing a meta-analysis of North American patients, concludes, "The few studies that examined suicidal ideation before and after gender transition found suicidal ideation to be increased." This study follows Kenneth J. Zucker, Anne A. Lawrence, and Baudewijntje P.C. Kreukels, "Gender Dysphoria in Adults," *Annual Review of Clinical Psychology* (2016), 12:217-247, who say "Sex reassignment is associated with more serious psychological sequelae and more prevalent regret than had previously been supposed" (p237).

Piece 5: "How Long Has He Been Like This?"

1 Evans and Evans, *Gender Dysphoria*, 93.
2 John Calvin, Calvin's Commentaries (1852; reprint, Grand Rapids, MI: Baker, 1981), XVI:II:322.

3 Walt Heyer, *Trans Life Survivors* (Walt Heyer, 2018), 94.
4 "...It may be that the [gender dysphoria] has emerged as secondary to another, more 'primary' psychiatric disorder, such as autism spectrum disorder, or borderline personality disorder, or as a result of a severe trauma (e.g., sexual abuse). In such situations, it could be argued that the [gender dysphoria] would dissipate if the more primary condition were treated." Kenneth J. Zucker, "Gender dysphoria in children and adolescents," in Kathryn S. K. Hall & Yitzchak M. Binik, editors, *Principles and practices of sex therapy* (6th ed.), (New York: The Guilford Press, 2020), 411. As cited earlier {Piece 1, p18-19}, British therapists Dr. Susan Evans and Dr. Marcus Evans practice with such a trauma model.

Piece 6: Sometimes We Are Wrong About Ourselves

1 Mary Charles McNeil, Edward A. Polloway and J. David Smith, "Feral and Isolated Children: Historical Review and Analysis," *Education and Training of the Mentally Retarded*, Vol. 19, No. 1 (February, 1984), 71-75. In most cases, reclaimed children never learn to speak and remain plagued by mental atrophy and asociality for the rest of their natural lives.
2 Sam A. Andreades, *Dating with Discernment* (Minneapolis, MN: Cruciform Press, 2021), 61-72, gives a brief treatment of how, for example, men and women in relationship are an image of the Trinity.
3 Paul McHugh, "Transgender Surgery Isn't the Solution," *The Wall Street Journal*, June 12, 2014. Dr. McHugh leveled this criticism while still Psychiatrist in Chief at the University. But he made the comparison over twenty years earlier, in Paul McHugh, "Psychiatric Misadventures," The American Scholar 61, no. 4 (1992); 502-503.
4 Sam A. Andreades, *enGendered* (Bellingham, WA: Lexham Press, 2015), 50-57, gives an exposition of the Bible's talk of gender in terms of relationship.

Piece 7: The Way Home

1 John Calvin, *Institutes of the Christian Religion in Two Volumes*, John T. McNeill editor, Ford Lewis Battles translator (Philadelphia, PA: The Westminster Press, 1960), I:37.
2 Corrie Ten Boom with Elizabeth & John Sherrill, *The Hiding Place -35th Anniversary Edition* (Grand Rapids, MI: Chosen Books, 2006), "Ravensbruck," 235.
3 Martin Hengel, *Crucifixion* (Philadelphia, PA: Fortress Press, 1977), 87.
4 Ibid., 28, 33-38, 87-88.
5 Pro Rabirio V.16, as cited in Ibid., 42.

Piece 9: Rediscovering Gender

1 Figures from Jeffrey M. Jones, "LGBT Identification in U.S. Ticks Up to 7.1%," February 17, 2022, Gallup.com.
2 I say, "was" because England's National Health System shut down the GIDS in the spring of 2023 after a high-profile lawsuit highlighted the lack of scientific evidence for the safety and efficacy of the chemical and surgical measures routinely used. After the British NHS announcement, Scotland, Sweden and Finland also suspended such treatment for minors. The American government and med-

ical establishment, however, soldier on.
3 N.M. de Graaf, G. Giovanardi, C. Zitz, et al., "Sex Ratio in Children and Adolescents Referred to the Gender Identity Development Service in the UK (2009–2016)," *Archives of Sexual Behavior* 47 (2018): 1301–1304.
4 GIDS website.
5 Andreades, *enGendered*, 50-57.
6 Out of the 85 uses of the English word *female* in the English Standard Version of the Bible, the word occurs 67 times with *male* within the space of five verses.
7 For example, a 2013 study at the University of Louisville found rates of depression and anxiety "far surpass the rates of those for the general population:" Stephanie L Budge, Jill L Adelson, Kimberly A S Howard, "Anxiety and depression in transgender individuals: the roles of transition status, loss, social support, and coping," *Journal of Consulting and Clinical Psychology*, June, 2013; 81(3):545-57. Some argue that society's expectations create these conditions. But results are quite mixed as to whether the conditions desist long-term after living as the opposite gender.
8 Katy Steinmetz, "Elliot Page is Ready for This Moment," (*Time*: March 16, 2021).
9 Elisabeth Elliot, *The Mark of a Man* (Grand Rapids: Revell, a division of Baker Publishing Group, 1981), 56.

Piece 10: Valuing Woman

1 William L. Lane, *The Gospel According to Mark* (Grand Rapids: Eerdmans, 1974), 192, n45, 46.
2 In Mar 5:32, when Jesus "looked around to see who had done it," before He knew who it was, the article and participle Mark uses to describe the one Jesus is looking for is feminine. Some commentators argue that that feminine reference is just expressing the narrator's perspective, nothing more. This view is supported by the parallel, as Luke expresses the same question with the masculine (Luk 8:45). But others argue the possibility that Jesus, as indicated by Mark, knew that the power that left Him went to a womanly matter.
3 Catherine Hezser, *The Oxford Handbook of Jewish Daily Life in Roman Palestine* (Oxford: Oxford University Press, 2010), 333-334; Lane, *The Gospel of Mark* 197.
4 Among American girls today, the average age of menarche is 12 years old. Centers for Disease Control and Prevention's National Health and Nutrition Examination Survey data, Data file: P_RHO.xpt, Variable RHQ020: "Age range at first menstrual period," August, 2021. https://wwwn.cdc.gov/Nchs/Nhanes/2017-2018/P_RHQ.htm#RHD018

Piece 11: Beckoning Man

1 Andreades, *enGendered*, 81-131, and Andreades, *Dating with Discernment*, 87-150, 163-242, give a fuller exposition of this and the other asymmetries of relationship highlighted in this chapter.
2 If we accept the numbers given in Scripture, Jonathan was much older than David. Saul reigned 40 years (Act 13:21) and David was 30 years old when right after Saul he began to reign (2Sa 5:4). This means that David was born in the 10th year of Saul's reign. But Jonathan was already fighting (and winning) battles in the 3rd year of Saul's reign (1Sa 13:1, 3). Even if Jonathan was such an able soldier at age 18, by the time David is born, Jonathan would be at least 25. Which

places Jonathan in the category of uncle rather than peer and makes his support of David for the throne all the more striking.
3 Getty Images of North America: Justin Casterline/Getty Images Sport
4 Before competing as Lia Thomas, the swimmer competed as Will R. Thomas, as shown in this 2019 scoresheet for Men's Freestyle: Will R. Thomas. https://ivyleague.com/documents/2019/3/1/Day_Three_Finals_Results.pdf
5 I sketched this chart from the standard distribution data reported in Francois Bellemare, Alphonse Jeanneret, and Jacques Couture, "Sex Differences in Thoracic Dimensions and Configuration," *American Journal of Respiratory and Critical Care Medicine* Volume 168, Issue 3 (Aug 2003), 265-400.
6 Grant R. Osborne, *Revelation* (Grand Rapids, MI: Baker Academic, 2002), 462.

Piece 12: The Stutterer Orator

1 Waltke, *Genesis*, 262, so comments on her birth name given in Gen 17:15.

Piece 13: Psycho-Medical Science, History, and the History of the Science

1 "Transgender Health: An Endocrine Society Position Statement," accessed April 04, 2023. https://www.endocrine.org/advocacy/position-statements/transgender-health
2 Thomas D. Steensma, et al., "Desisting and persisting gender dysphoria after childhood: A qualitative follow-up study," *Clinical Child Psychology and Psychiatry*, 16:4 (2011), 499-516. The statement in the Introduction on p500 references a number of studies.
3 McHugh, "Transgender Surgery..." (2014) noted this high desistence rate. Jiska Ristori and Thomas D. Steensma, "Gender Dysphoria in Childhood," *International Review of Psychiatry* 28:1 (2016), 15, tabulated the ten studies done to date. Averaging the counts of all these studies yields the 85% gender dysphoria desistence rate. More recently, Stephen B. Levine, E. Abbruzzese & Julia W. Mason, "Reconsidering Informed Consent for Trans-Identified Children, Adolescents, and Young Adults," *Journal of Sex & Marital Therapy* 48:7 (2022), 711, said: "There have been eleven research studies to date indicating a high rate of resolution of gender incongruence in children by late adolescence or young adulthood without medical interventions...An attempt has been made to discount the applicability of this research, suggesting that the studies were based on merely gender non-conforming, rather than truly gender-dysphoric, children... However, a reanalysis of the data prompted by this critique confirmed the initial finding: Among children meeting the diagnostic criteria for "Gender Identity Disorder" in DSM-IV (currently "Gender Dysphoria" in DSM-5), 67% were no longer gender-dysphoric as adults; the rate of natural resolution for gender dysphoria was 93% for children whose gender dysphoria was significant but subthreshold for the DSM diagnosis...."
4 E.g., "I would like to point out that identifying in any way is optional, it's personal and it's subject to change," Ashley, Wylde, "Changing the Way You Identify," YouTube, May 9, 2016, Timestamp 0:13. https://www.youtube.com/watch?v=YZY7kkYzWI
5 Aruna Saraswat, Megan Weinand, Joshua D. Safer "Evidence Supporting the Biologic Nature of Gender Identity," *Endocrine Practice* 21:2 (Feb, 2015): 199-204;

Stephen M. Rosenthal, "Approach to the Patient: Transgender Youth: Endocrine Considerations," *The Journal of Clinical Endocrinology & Metabolism* Volume 99, Issue 12 (December, 2014): 4379–4389.
6 I provide a summary in the text. My more complete two-part digest may be found here: https://affirminggender.com/2018/05/03/strange-science-in-the-service-of-a-statement/
7 Sarah-Jayne Blakemore, Stephanie Burnett, and Ronald E. Dah, "The Role of Puberty in the Developing Adolescent Brain," *Human Brain Mapping* 31 (2010):926. The study is an example of the brain changing through hormonal activity during adolescence.
8 Saraswat, et al., 200.
9 L. Simon, L.R. Kozák, V. Simon, P. Czobor, Z. Unoka, Á. Szabó, G. Csukly, "Regional grey matter structure differences between transsexuals and healthy controls--a voxel based morphometry study," *PLoS One* 8:12 (Dec 31, 2013):e83947.
10 Saraswat, et al., 201.
11 Rosenthal, 4383.
12 Andrew Scull, *Desperate Remedies: Psychiatry's Turbulent Quest to Cure Mental Illness* (Cambridge, MA: Harvard University Press, 2022).
13 Ibid., 34.
14 Ibid., 35.
15 Ibid., 75, 91.
16 Ibid., 92-97.
17 Ibid., 99-109.
18 Walt Heyer, *Paper Genders* (Make Waves Publishing, 2011), 47-63, draws the comparison between lobotomies and current so-called gender-affirming care.
19 Scull, *Desperate Remedies*, 135-187.

Piece 14: Battling Against the Body

1 Grandview Research.com, accessed March 25, 2023: "The U.S. sex reassignment surgery market size was valued at USD 1.9 billion in 2021 and is expected to expand at a compound annual growth rate (CAGR) of 11.23% from 2022 to 2030." https://www.grandviewresearch.com/industry-analysis/us-sex-reassignment-surgery-market?utm_source=substack&utm_medium=email
2 Joyce, *Trans*, pp232-233, gives the approximate prices in 2021.
3 RJM Cumming, K. Sylvester, and J Fuld, "Understanding the effects on lung function of chest binder use in the transgender population," *Thorax* 71 (2016) (Suppl 3):A227, found "abnormal lung function." Sarah Peitzmeier, et al., "Health impact of chest binding among transgender adults: a community-engaged, cross-sectional study," *Culture, Health & Sexuality* 19:1 (2017), 64-75, surveyed 1,800 chest-binding women and found 97% reported negative health effects, including pain, lung problems, and rib fractures.
4 Denise Vink, Joost Rotteveel, and Daniel Klink, "Bone Mineral Density in Adolescents with Gender Dysphoria During Prolonged Gonadotropin Releasing Hormone Analog Treatment," World Professional Association for Transgender Health (symposium presentation, 2016), found that the children undergoing puberty suppression fell behind the average rates of bone-density growth for their age. Mariska C. Vlot, et al., "Effect of pubertal suppression and cross-sex hormone therapy on bone turnover markers and bone mineral apparent density (BMAD) in transgender adolescents," *Bone* 95 (2017): 11–19, also found that puberty suppressors decreased bone growth.

5 E.g., Maiko A. Schneider, et al., "Brain Maturation, Cognition and Voice Pattern in a Gender Dysphoria Case under Pubertal Suppression," *Frontiers in Human Neuroscience* 11 (November, 2017), 1, using MRI scans and memory tests, detected a degradation in cognitive performance in an individual during puberty suppression.

6 Note Dr. Rosenthal's continued stress on informed consent of the patient about to get puberty blockers concerning the risks of infertility: Rosenthal, "Approach to the Patient...", 4380, 4385, 4386-4387. Given that teens who begin on puberty blockers continue invariably to cross-sex hormones a few years later, their inability to bear children becomes almost guaranteed.

7 These include increased risk of heart attacks, diabetes, stroke, blood clots, and endometrial cancer.

8 Andrea Long Chu, "My New Vagina Won't Make Me Happy: And it shouldn't have to," New York Times *Opinion*, Nov 24, 2018.

9 Lila Shapiro, "Andrea Long Chu Wants More," *Vulture*, October 16, 2019.

10 Leonard Sax gives an up-to-date, book-length treatment of some significant sex differences between men and women in Leonard Sax, *Why Gender Matters: What Parents and Teachers Need to Know about the Emerging Science of Sex Differences*, Second Edition (New York: Harmony Books, 2017).

11 "Mapping sex-differential gene expression we found more than 6500 protein-coding genes with significant sex differentiated expression in one tissue or more." Moran Gershoni & Shmuel Pietrokovski, "The landscape of sex-differential transcriptome and its consequent selection in human adults," *BMC Biology*, February 07, 2017; 15:7. The Weizmann Institute of Science also published a helpful digest, https://wis-wander.weizmann.ac.il/life-sciences/researchers-identify-6500-genes-are-expressed-differently-men-and-women

Piece 15: A Message to the Church: The Last Shall Be First

1 E.g., Sam A. Andreades, "What ex-gay men can teach us about marriage," *World Magazine*, June 29, 2013.

2 CampusPride.org keeps a complete, updated list at: https://www.campuspride.org/tpc/student-health-insurance/

3 "Healthcare Laws and Policies: Medicaid Coverage for Transgender-Related Health Care," movement advancement project, April 12, 2023. https://www.lgbtmap.org/equality-maps/medicaid

Conclusion

1 Nancy Pearcey, *Love Thy Body: Answering Hard Questions about Life and Sexuality* (Grand Rapids, MI: BakerBooks, 2018); Carl Trueman, *The Rise and Triumph of the Modern Self: Cultural Amnesia, Expressive Individualism, and the Road to Sexual Revolution* (Wheaton, Il: Crossway, 2020).

2 Queer Theory's rather explicit goal, developing through the latter part of the twentieth century, was to disrupt the structures of family by breaking down all categories of gender in relationship. Michael Warner was a leading general at Yale in this charge for the destruction with books like: Michael Warner, ed., *Fear of a Queer Planet: Queer Politics and Social Theory* (Minneapolis, MN: University of Minnesota Press, 1993); Michael Warner, *The Trouble with Normal: Sex,*

Politics, and the Ethics of Queer Life (Cambridge, MA: Harvard University Press, 1999). Ms. Joyce gives a lucid popular exposition of the queer ideology in Joyce, *Trans*, 1-70.
3 Andreades, *Dating with Discernment*, 62-72, 256-262.
4 Andreades, *enGendered*, 150-154.
5 Andreades, *enGendered*, 155-165.

Bible Book Name Abbreviations

1Ch	1 Chronicles	Hos	Hosea
1Co	1 Corinthians	Isa	Isaiah
1Jo	1 John	Jer	Jeremiah
1Ki	1 Kings	Jam	James
1Pe	1 Peter	Jdg	Judges
1Sa	1 Samuel	Job	Job
1Th	1 Thessalonians	Joe	Joel
1Ti	1 Timothy	Joh	John
2Ch	2 Chronicles	Jon	Jonah
2Co	2 Corinthians	Jos	Joshua
2Jo	2 John	Jud	Jude
2Ki	2 Kings	Lam	Lamentations
2Pe	2 Peter	Lev	Leviticus
2Sa	2 Samuel	Luk	Luke
2Th	2 Thessalonians	Mal	Malachi
2Ti	2 Timothy	Mar	Mark
3Jo	3 John	Mat	Matthew
Act	Acts	Mic	Micah
Amo	Amos	Nah	Nahum
Col	Colossians	Neh	Nehemiah
Dan	Daniel	Num	Numbers
Deu	Deuteronomy	Oba	Obadiah
Ecc	Ecclesiastes	Phi	Philippians
Eph	Ephesians	Phm	Philemon
Est	Esther	Pro	Proverbs
Exo	Exodus	Psa	Psalms
Eze	Ezekiel	Rev	Revelation
Ezr	Ezra	Rom	Romans
Gal	Galatians	Rut	Ruth
Gen	Genesis	Sos	Song of Solomon
Hab	Habakkuk	Tiu	Titus
Hag	Haggai	Zec	Zechariah
Heb	Hebrews	Zep	Zephaniah

Index of Scriptures Referenced

	Verses	Page(s)
Genesis		
	1-2	12
	1:26-27	56
	1:27	81, 132, 139
	2:7	25, 35, 69, 93, 135
	2:15	93
	2:24	140
	2:25	12, 42
	3	43
	3:7	43
	3:10-11	43
	3:11	50, 52
	3:16	91
	3:21	52, 64
	5:1-2	132, 139
	11:30	104, 107
	15:5	104
	16:1-2	132
	17:4	104
	17:5	104
	17:15-19	105
	17:15	148
	17:17	107
	18:6-8	105
	18:11	107
	18:12	105
	21:1-7	106
	21:5	107
	22:17	104
	24	104
	25:20	107
	25:21	104, 105, 106, 107
	25:26	107
	26:4	104
	29:20	107
	29:31	104
	30:1-2	105, 107
	30:20	107
	30:22-25	106, 107
	31:38	107
	32:12	104
	35:11	104
Exodus		
	3:11-4:13	132
	4-19	104
	4:10	104
	7:7	107
	20:16	57
Leviticus		
	19:18	74
Numbers		
	12:3-8	104
Deuteronomy		
	4:16	81
	22:5	27
	32:21	139
Joshua		
	24:15	13-14
Judges		
	2:11-15	139
	6:1-6	59
	6:11-12	59
	6:11	59
	6:13-17	59
	11:28-40	90
Ruth		
	2:8-16	93
1Samuel		
	1:1-3	93
	1:3	93
	1:25-28	93
	2:10-36	93
	2:26	94
	3:1-21	93
	3:1-10	93-94

153

3:1	95	*Ecclesiastes*	
3:3	95	5:18	73
3:8-9	95	*Song of Songs*	
4:1	93	2:7	75
4:11	93	3:5	75
13:1-3	147	8:4	75
17:26	96	*Isaiah*	
17:34-35	96	7:14	101
18:1-5	96	19:1	139
19:7	96	28:14-19	50
20:1-42	96	53:1-12	66
23:16-18	96	66:7	101

2Samuel		*Jeremiah*	
5:4	147	1:4-5	59
7	93	1:6	59

2Chronicles		1:7-8	60
36:12	59	25:1-14	139

Ezra		*Amos*	
1:1	59	6:14	139

Job		*Micah*	
5:7	78	5:3-4	101
30:20	139		

Psalms			
104:3	139		

Proverbs		*Matthew*	
1:8-10	16	5-7	37
1:15	16	5:36	37-38
4:1-4	31	9:18-26	88
4:10-19	16	9:21	92
5:1-23	16	17:15	49
6:20-24	16	19:26	100
7:1-5	16	20:16	129, 133
8:22-31	140	24:19	89
19:2	73	*Mark*	
23:15-17	16	5:21-43	88
23:19-22	16	5:25	89
23:26-27	16	5:26	88
24:13-22	16	5:30	89
28:7	16	5:32	147
		5:39	89
		5:41	91

Index of Scriptures Referenced

5:42	89	12:22-25	129-130
5:43	92	12:24	130-131
9:14-29	47-49	12:27	56
9:14	49	15:1-17	36
9:18-19	49	15:12-23	36
9:18	49	15:48-54	36
9:20	49	*Galatians*	
9:21	49, 52	6:1	14-15
9:22-24	49	*Ephesians*	
9:28-29	49	1:20-21	139
10:31	129, 133	2:19	64
13:17	89	3:14-17	56, 140

Luke

		4:15	15, 23
1:26-30	60	4:28	75
1:31-36	60	5:22-33	140
7:11-15	89	6:4	31
7:47	132	*Philippians*	
8:41-56	88	2:9	139
8:42	90	*Colossians*	
8:43	90	1:18	36
13:6-9	106	1:21-22	65-66, 68, 128
13:30	129, 133	2:10	139
19:1-9	60	3:10	64
23:27-31	89	3:21	31

John

		1 Timothy	
3:8	133	3:1-2	93
15:13-14	64	*Titus*	

Acts

		1:5-9	93
13:21	147	*Philemon*	
26:9-18	60	1:1-25	60

Romans

		Hebrews	
1:21-32	28	11:32-34	59
7:14-20	78	13:4	71, 75
7:15-23	73	*James*	
8:11	36	1:3	137
8:28	103	1:6	137
12:5	56	1:13-17	72

1 Corinthians

		1:14	75
1:27-28	133	1:15	74
11:3	93, 140	2:1	137
11:12	140	2:5	137

155

2:14-26	136
2:14	137
2:17	136
2:21-25	137
2:26	136
4:7	18

1Peter

3:22	139
5:8-9	18

2John

1:1	103

Revelation

1:5	36
12:1-10	100-101
12:1-7	111
12:5	101, 102
12:9-11	101

Made in the USA
Columbia, SC
11 April 2025